Follow the Leader
A Dog's-Eye View of Washington DC

Follow the Leader
A Dog's-Eye View of Washington DC

as told to M. Vincent

Eastbank Publishing
Washington, DC

Eastbank Publishing Co.
325 Pennsylvania Avenue, SE
Washington, DC 20003
email: book@firstdog.com
202-337-7898

© 2000 M. Vincent and Eastbank Publishing.

All rights reserved. No part of this book may be reproduced or transmitted in any form
or by any means, electronic or mechanical, including photocopying, recording, or by any information
storage and retrieval system, without permission in writing from the publisher.

Library of Congress Cataloging-in-publication available on request.

ISBN 0-9670911-0-1 (Paper back)
ISBN 0-9670911-1-X (Hard Cover)

First edition
Printed in the USA by Colortone Press

Photographic credits appear on page 114

Computer Graphics Ted Christensen and Cheryl Mohrmann
Cover Design Communication & Design

Acknowledgments

To photographer, Lynn Bogert Dykstra of Focused Images Photography, Inc., whose photographs inspired this book; to Webmaster Theodore Christensen, who used her pictures and others to build my web site (www.firstdog.com); to Florice Whyte Kovan of Academic and Publishers Research, who located archival photos; to Ben Man who provided scenic Watergate photographs from his private collection; to photographers Alan Porter, P.F. Bentley, Harry Benson, Michael J. N. Bowles, Eddie Adams, Cameron Davidson and Deborah Feingold, whose works contribute greatly to this book; to Brian Culp, Dole Archivist at the University of Kansas, for providing photographs from the Robert J. Dole Collection.

A Prayer for the Animals

Albert Schweitzer

Hear our humble prayer, O God,
For our friends the animals.
Especially for animals who are suffering;
For any that are hunted or lost or
Deserted or frightened or hungry;
For all that must be put to death.
We entreat for them all thy mercy
And pity. And for those who deal
With them, we ask a heart
Of compassion, gentle and kindly words.
Make us true friends of
The animals and so to share
The blessings of the merciful.

The Washington Humane Society

is the only welfare organization chartered by Congress (1870). At that time the main focus was on draft horses, like the ones below. Today, humane law enforcement, education, and adoption programs serve all of the city's furred, feathered and finned residents.

Proceeds from this book will be donated to The Washington Humane Society

To Bob and Elizabeth Dole,
who saved my life,
and to my buddy, Wilbert Jones.

CONTENTS

My Journey   12

Discover Leader as a shelter foundling who moves—literally overnight—to a Watergate apartment and a position of prominence in Washington. See his skillful rise to power, as he is crowned Chair Dog of the Bark Ball and named Mr. September for the Ralston Purina Calendar. Meet Leader's media mentors: Larry King, Willard Scott, Jay Leno and David Letterman. Learn why General Hugh Shelton and General (Ret.) Barry McCaffrey recommend Leader to the CIA.

My Hometown   46

Introduced by Mayor Anthony Williams, this section features fifteen color photos of Leader's tour of Washington's monuments, from the Lincoln Memorial to Cedar Hill, the Frederick Douglass Home in Anacostia.

Leader offers personal commentary at each sight, but learns from Einstein at his Memorial that "Politics is for the moment, an equation is for eternity."

1996 Presidential Paw Poll

Leader 55% Socks 44%

My Internet Victory   78

In America's first national election via the World Wide Web, Leader's battle with Socks is a "Fight For the Run of the White House," according to the *Baltimore Sun*. Leader easily defeats the Arkansas tom cat by the widest margin ever recorded for any White House candidate.

"Masterpiece of a home page," an e-mail from Norway, is a typical response from Leader's enthusiastic supporters. Therein lies the secret to his victory, and why his site (firstdog.com) is still one of the most popular net stops.

My Watergate Days   97

Inevitably, Leader becomes a movie star when he is recruited to portray himself in the biography of Leader Dole. The film, **The Political Animal**, receives rave reviews when it is telecast on USA Network, preceding its annual live broadcast of the Westminster Kennel Club Dog Show from Madison Square Garden.

This section features the beauty of Leader's playground at the Watergate, through its changing seasons, with scenes that any Hollywood set designer would envy.

Greetings...

With pen to paw, now having attained and passed the age of 17 years, I, Leader Dole, herein record the journey of my life.

It was my good fortune to have been born with a keen sense of sight and sound far beyond that possessed by any human and to have observed for 15 years, close-up and with "furbatim" recall, Washington's political, social and cultural scene.

I wish to share with you the personal adventures I have experienced, which began behind bars at the D.C. Animal Shelter and ended up in the inner sanctums of the Washington power structure.

Follow me.

Washington, D. C.
January 1999

My Journey

From the Shelter...

No one knows how I came to be found on New York Avenue in Washington, D.C. and taken to the Animal Shelter, but there I was -- no ID tags, no collar, no future. I spent six days there and came within 24 hours of being put to sleep. It was the last week in November, 1984.

As soon as they locked the cage door, I knew I was in trouble. And like anyone in trouble, what I wanted most was OUT.

Barking and growling ferociously at the outrage of my jailing got me nowhere fast. My next move was to look for an opening to dig or wiggle my way out. But I was too small to climb over the

. . .to the Watergate!

top, and the concrete floor was too hard for my little paws. The opening between the bars of the cage was just wide enough to put my nose and part of my chin through, but not large enough for any more of me.

Another more ominous dilemma soon developed: after my first meal, I found myself bonding with my hosts. Somehow, the need to escape diminished with each morsel.

From my stall near the doorway, I was able to watch the attendants bring in newcomers and also see the lucky current occupants walking out with their new owners. My first Washington parade -- and I had a front row seat!

Before I go any further, I need to point out that I am a miniature schnauzer. My guess is that I was raised by a breeder because I had never before seen any dog other than a miniature schnauzer. Here, there were small dogs with long hair -- as well as big dogs with short hair -- some with short noses, like mine, but others with long or wide noses; ears long and floppy or short and pointed; some tails stubby, like mine, but others long and hanging down. One stuck-up dog had a tail that went straight up in the air, with long hair cascading down in a circle like an open parasol. Some had tight-fitting skin, like a glove; others had skin so loose it hung on them in layers.

It was not only that they looked different; they all sounded different when they barked. Schnauzers have a pleasant but serious bark, and once our message is heard, we at least try to stop. The big dogs had a throaty confident bark, which they expressed sparingly, but the smaller dogs never seemed to stop yelping, like the world was coming to an end.

Many times, I would look up and see strangers pressing their heads close to the cages to get a better look inside.

They had small pads to scribble notes, their heads moving back and forth from the note pad to the dog. They would stop briefly, then move quickly to a nearby cage, apparently sure of what they wanted and determined to find it.

Who would have thought that a vote on the floor of the U.S. Senate would mean the difference between life and death for me, a miniature schnauzer identified as #1498 at the Washington Animal Shelter.

Across town, Elizabeth Dole, then Secretary of Transportation, was meeting with the Federal Aviation Administrator. When the door suddenly burst open, Shirley Ballard's smile required no explanation. Elizabeth knew it signaled that Bob Dole - - facing 4 opponents and after a cliff hanger on the fifth ballot - - had been elected Senate Majority Leader of the 99th Congress.

She had planned to give Bob a dog, a small fluffy one, for his Christmas present. But she decided that this was the right moment and said to her assistant, Charlotte Ellis, "Let's get the dog right now. Let's give it to him today... and we'll name it LEADER."

Within the hour, fate brought Charlotte Ellis to my cage, and I heard her say to the attendant at her side, "I'm looking for a small dog like this one." Her eyes met mine. Then, she walked over to the pay phone, and I heard her say, "Elizabeth, I've found Bob's present. Yes, a miniature schnauzer -- gray and white. He's perfect. I know you'll like him. He's so beautiful!" I have to admit feeling flattered.

The attendant added, "He's very well behaved. We don't see many schnauzers here, and his time is up tomorrow.

15

"No one had to draw me a picture; I knew what "his time is up" meant.

Charlotte took charge, and before I could say "Bow Wow!" she had made all the arrangements for my release. The shelter staff was as happy to see me leave as I was to go. After they gave me a nice bath, and dried me off, I walked out with Charlotte, ready to start my new life and hoping that no one could see my fur stand on end when I thought about how close I had come to not being here.

My first stop was the Senate Office Building on Capitol Hill where a press conference was being held to announce Bob Dole's election as Majority Leader. I waited outside in the hall and met Elizabeth for the first time. She attached the name tag "Leader" to my collar and lovingly picked me up. Then, cradling me in her arms, she entered the room, where I was presented to a surprised but smiling Bob. People were standing wall to wall, some with cameras or down on one knee with note pads -- all smiling and talking at the same time, sounding like a room full of bees. It was obvious that "Canine Leader Meets Senate Leader" was not on the agenda.

Surprised at the sight of me, Bob Dole smiled broadly as he realized that I was about to join the family. Everyone was looking at the three of us. Bob did have one important question for his wife, "Are we allowed to have dogs at the Watergate?" Elizabeth had the answer, and I loved it: "I don't know, but if we can't, we'll just have to move."

Wow! What difference a day makes!

I didn't know what Bob's job was, but I noticed right away that what he said would sometimes be interrupted by laughter, other times by applause, and many times by both laughter and applause.

HOME, AT LAST!

What a lucky puppy! I've found love, happiness and a perfect name – LEADER. **LEADER DOLE!**

17

In the Spotlight

On this day, I had no idea where my life was going. In contrast to an undocumented puppyhood, my new life was beginning to be just the opposite – cameras taking pictures of my every twist and turn, reporters writing notes about the color of my fur, the cut of my ears, the fuzz on my feet, the size of my stubby tail, the sound of my bark – nothing was off the record.

MEET THE PRESS

All the attention would have toppled the unprepared; however, schnauzers are born for the limelight, especially this overnight, rags-to-riches, bulb-flashing, in-your-face type. Schnauzers can handle sudden fame without getting big headed.

Working Like a Dog

Right away, I could see that I had a big job to do and had to get to work on time. It was easy for me to step up to the task because a schnauzer naturally expects to take on important responsibilities.

ON THE JOB POSING FOR A NEWS PHOTO

At first, it was enough for me just to show up around 8:30 a.m., greet the receptionist who hung my leash on the rack, check out the water bowl, then await my orders.

These assignments in the beginning were primarily social: posing for pictures with visitors, solo photos of the Leader's LEADER on the Capitol grounds. Or the "gimme your paw" thing, which I could do left or right, an uncommon trait not found in all breeds.

Much to my dismay, I soon concluded that security in Bob's office was minimal. Outside, Capitol Police with K-9's patrolled, but no one was protecting inside our offices, especially around the desks and windows. I put my best paw forward and volunteered to guard the office so everyone else could work without fear.

From strategic positions, I would walk my beat, carefully observe and report any breach. A few co-workers, through no fault of their own, objected to my method of communicating. They just didn't understand that I wasn't barking. I was "reporting." It didn't help matters that, unlike the Capitol Police, I was denied a uniform or badge to validate my activities. Nevertheless, the increasing importance of my job added to my self-esteem, and facing a few complainers was a small price I was willing to pay. Besides, I love to watch people work; watching is my favorite pastime.

On the Road with Wilbert

For 12 years, I travelled along the Mall to the U.S. Capitol with Bob or to the Department of Labor or Department of Transportation with Elizabeth.

Wilbert Jones at the Wheel

Whether I went to work with Bob or Elizabeth, we always took the same route along Constitution Avenue, where I first saw many of the monuments that I later would document with typical tourist photographs.

Wilbert Jones was always in the drivers seat. He and I would often be parked, while awaiting Bob's return from a meeting or waiting for Elizabeth and Bob to arrive at the airport. He could pass the time reading a newspaper, but it was pretty boring for me to wait around and twiddle my paws. So I devised a game of peek-a-boo.

From my cushion on the passenger seat, I would stare up at Wilbert as he turned the pages until his eyes met mine. At that split second, I would turn my head away, gazing innocently off into

21

space, pretending to ignore Wilbert, who would eventually ask, "Is there something you want to say to me, little man?" Like a sphinx, I kept staring out the window as if I hadn't

IN STEP AND ALL SMILES ON THE MORNING AFTER 1994 ELECTIONS

heard a word. Wilbert would return to his reading, knowing that before long I would start the game all over again.

22

As the Majority Leader, Bob had an office in the U.S. Capitol. But as the senior Senator from Kansas, he also had an office and another staff in the Hart Senate Office Building across the street. It was there in Room 141 that I set up my home base: an extremely comfortable, oval-shaped polka dot bed. A large number of staffers and interns were always volunteering to take me for walks.

WATCHING PEOPLE WORK

I liked to think they volunteered because I was so cute. But they probably volunteered because they liked the fresh air and exercise as much as I did.

It is well known that schnauzers are good watch dogs; regardless of what you may have heard, this is not merely accidental but based on our keen instincts and a natural curiosity. You know, the thing that killed the c-a-t.

One day, when a group of Boy Scouts visited Bob's office, I became more curious than usual. I had never seen so many small people together and wondered if there might be more where they came from. Tagging along, I followed them out the door and across the street to the capitol. At a certain point, I paused to check out a group of tourists listening to a lecture. When I looked around a few minutes later, the boy scouts were nowhere to be seen. Anyone familiar with the shape of the Capitol knows that it is round. And that's what I found myself doing – going round and round in circles.

I must admit that it was a bit disorienting. Soon I heard thundering footsteps, getting closer and closer, then someone shouting, "There he is, in the Rotunda!" After a brief period of captivity, the Capitol police handed me over to three of my friends from Bob's office, who had been dispatched to hunt me down.

Begging for snacks was my specialty, and Bob couldn't resist feeding me. He didn't always know it, but others were feeding me treats too. The office was such a large place that I could easily fill up by making the rounds, sometimes several times a day.

Unfortunately, my bulging stomach could not conceal my dietary transgressions; at this point, my name would change to "FATSO", and Bob would curtail my intake until the pot belly disappeared.

Fatso ?

Most callers had to have an appointment to see Bob, but if his office door was open, I knew I could walk in. If he was on the telephone, I would wait my turn. But when he saw me, he knew that whatever was on my mind had to be important. Like the time I requested an increase in my treat allowance.

P.F. Bentley, TIME photographer, recorded one of these meetings; so you can see how effective my negotiating skills can be when the subject is food.

CAN I HAVE MORE TREATS?

I'LL THINK ABOUT IT.

OKAY, YOU WIN.

25

DOT DAYS

20th Anniversary
1967 - 1987

When the Department of Transportation planned a program for their 20th Anniversary, Bob and I were asked to participate -- with one important condition -- we had to keep our entrance a secret because they wanted to surprise Elizabeth.

As you can see from the surprised look on her face, we succeeded.

Celebrating the Holidays

Modeling my yellow "slicky" raincoat, with the help of Shirley Ballard, Elizabeth, and Shirley Ybarra
(now Secretary of Virginia Department of Transportation).

"The more the merrier Christmas!"

Frequent Flyers...

Elizabeth and Bob have spent more time in the air than many full-time professional pilots. But flying high in the sky is not my idea of a fun thing to do, so I was glad to stay home, cross my paws, and wait for their return. When I met them here they were returning from an official overseas trip.

When Congress was in session, Bob would work long hours. While I was napping, he had to stand at a podium in the Senate to explain his position on issues or pay close attention to opposing views. It wasn't unusual for him to work until midnight and return to the office at 8:30 the next morning. Whatever his schedule, I stayed right with him, and I made sure that Wilbert did too.

Although he already had two demanding jobs, believe it or not, Bob took on a third challenge in 1988. He decided to run for President. He and Elizabeth had to travel even more, but when they did come home, I was there to meet them at the airport.

We didn't win but they said it was a wonderful experience.

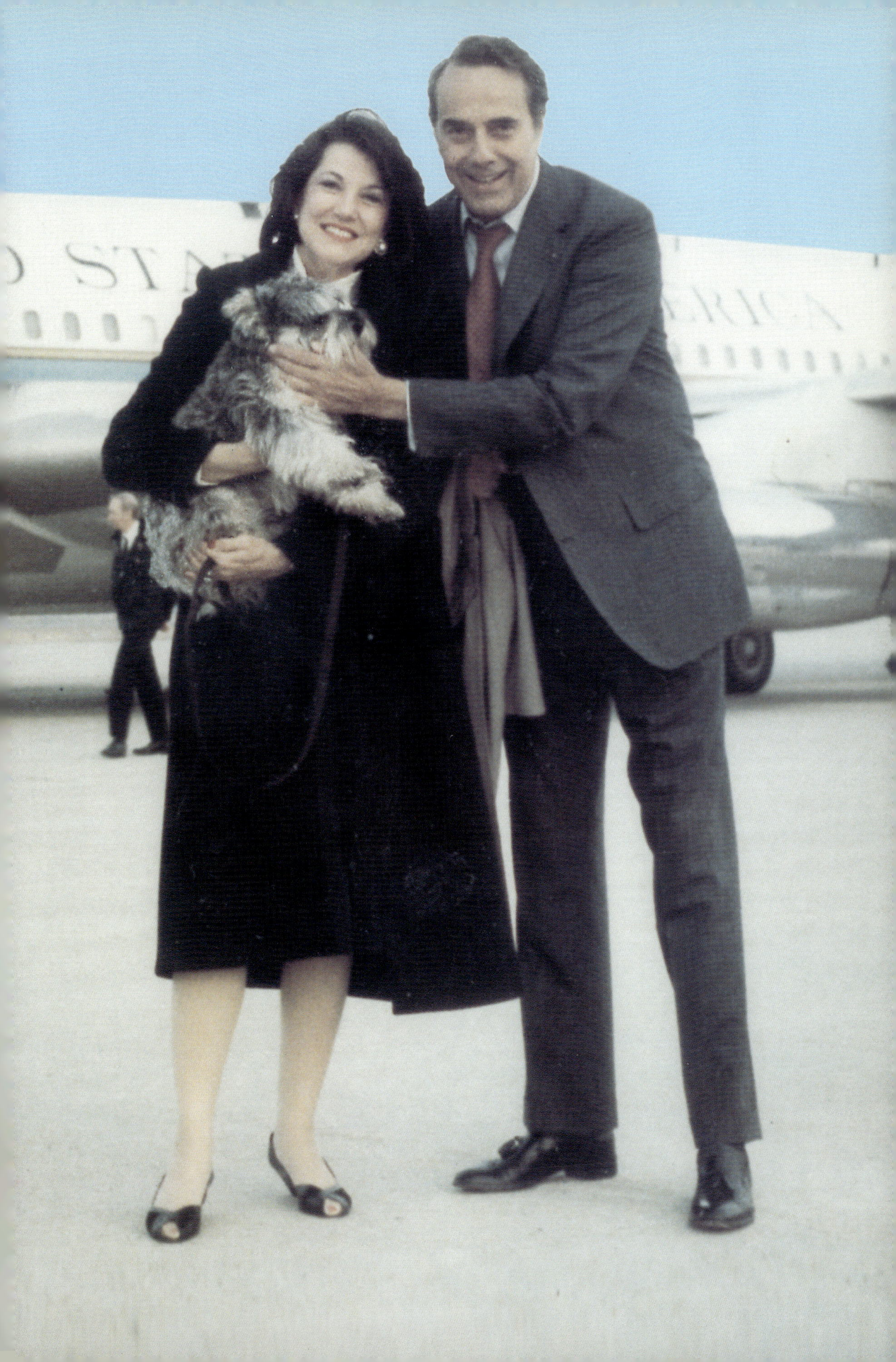

During election years, Bob was often out of town; as Majority Leader, he was in demand as a speaker for other candidates, and he returned home to Kansas frequently. On those days, I would accompany Elizabeth to her office, where again I was on guard duty. Regardless of where I "worked" my appearance at media events was becoming routine and sometimes "by request."

Photographer Laura Patterson caught me here...

Photographers were literally hounding me, taking pictures as I rode in the car and trying to catch me off guard.

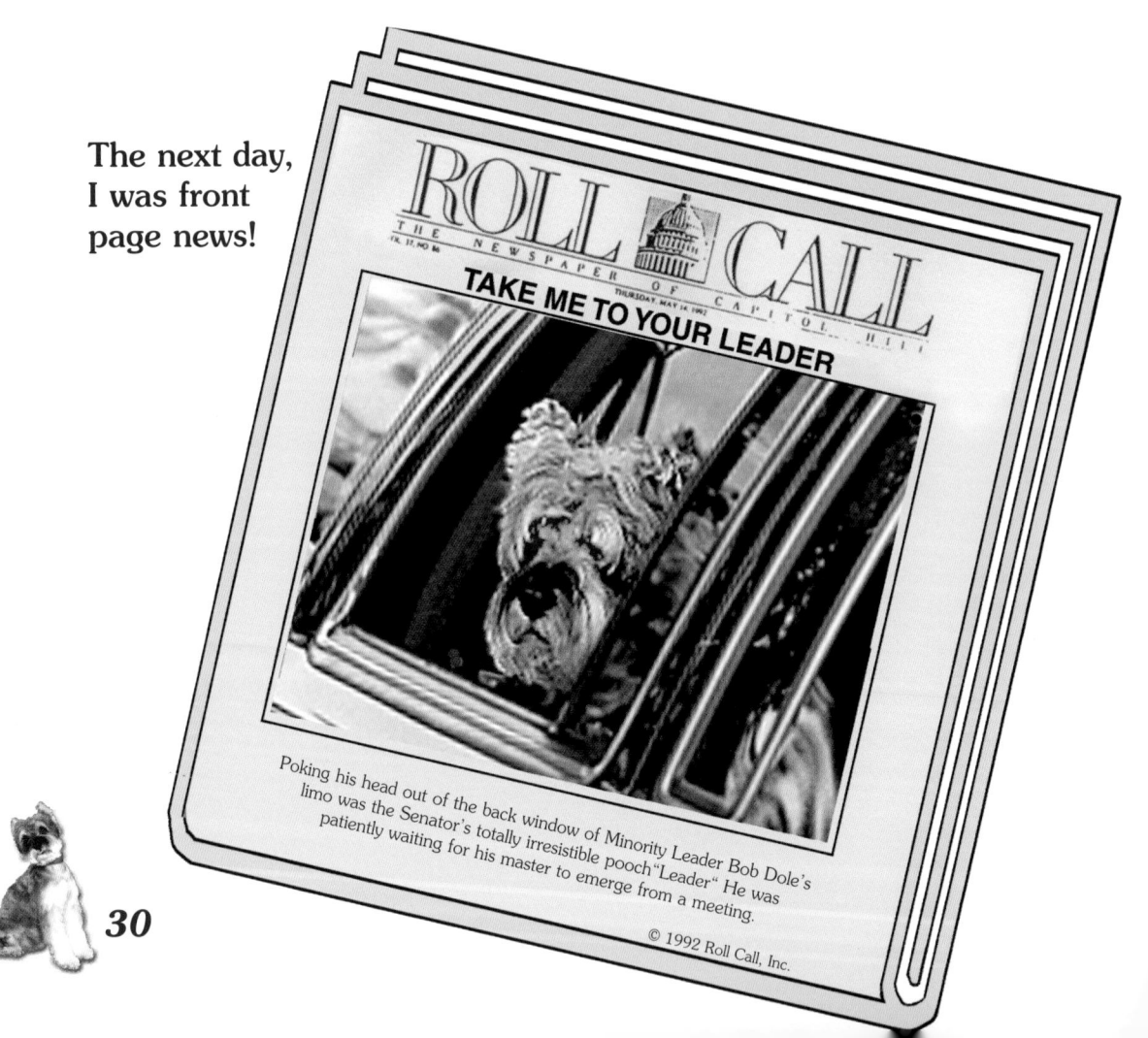

The next day, I was front page news!

ROLL CALL

TAKE ME TO YOUR LEADER

Poking his head out of the back window of Minority Leader Bob Dole's limo was the Senator's totally irresistible pooch "Leader." He was patiently waiting for his master to emerge from a meeting.

© 1992 Roll Call, Inc.

Soon, I was receiving requests to appear in national publications, like this one for PARADE magazine. I thought it would be nice to have Elizabeth and Bob in the picture too.

Going National — and in Color!

31

USA TODAY

NO. 1 IN THE USA... FIRST IN DAILY READERS

Taking a picture of me on the couch seemed like a good idea, but I almost fell asleep. Bob woke me just in time.

This family portrait appeared in Carolyn Mulford's book, "Elizabeth Dole, Public Servant."

**Leader gets a prominent place
in a portrait of the Doles**

33

TV GUIDE

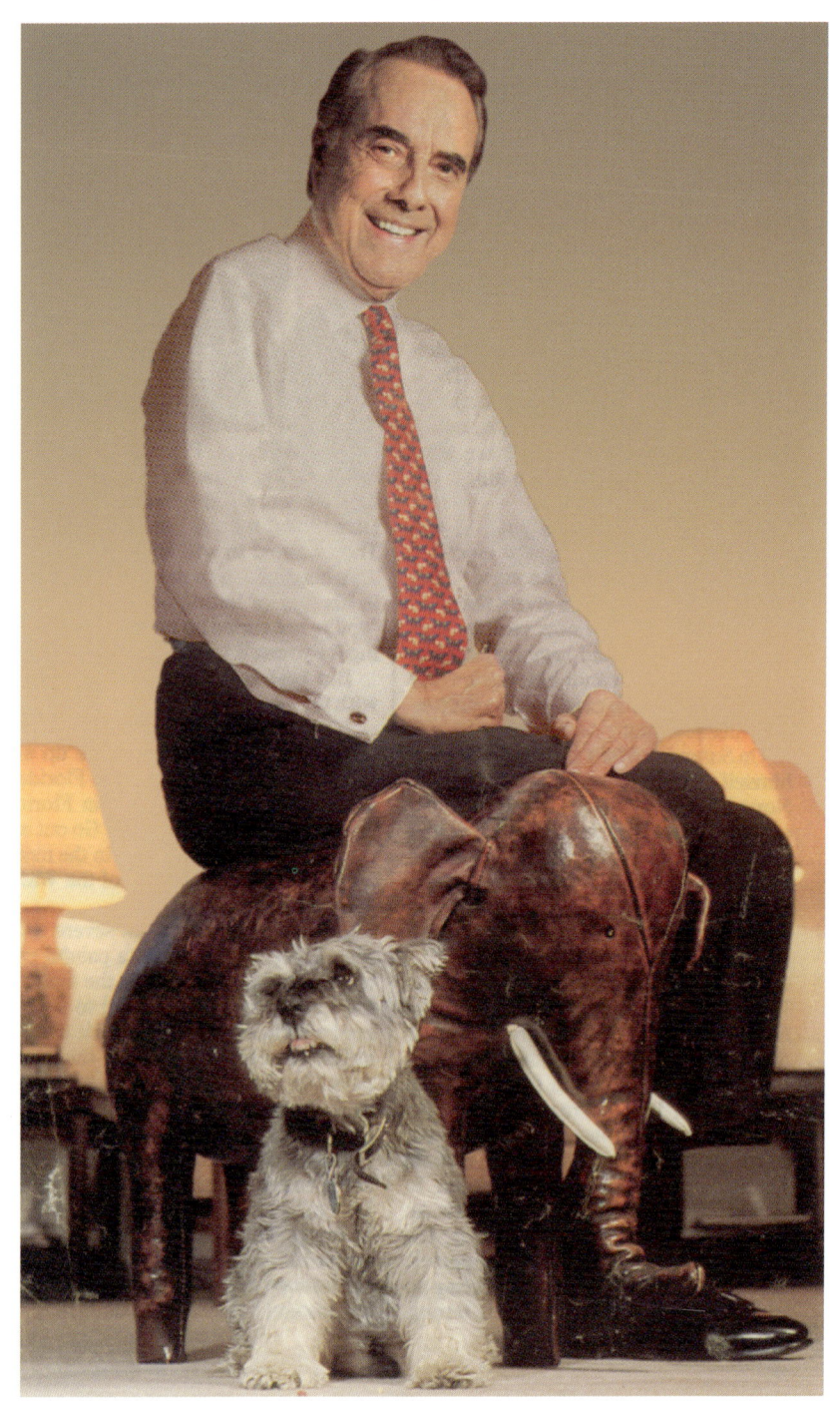

#1 Sidekick

34

Newsweek

United we stand

35

THE KING AND I

Normally, I'm not a name-dropper, but I do know Larry King. If you want to learn to be a talk show host, watch him. He's the best!

He taught me a lot and let me watch close up how he works. When you become a Washington celebrity, you never know when you might be called for a television appearance.

Fortunately, I was ready when the phone started ringing off the hook. Larry King one day, David Letterman the next.

When it comes to watching television, I'm a real couch potato. One of my favorites is Jay Leno's *Tonight Show*. I almost fell out of my bed one night when Elizabeth rode in on the back of Jay's motorcycle.

David Letterman is another of my regulars. On this show, he spoke about Bob's book *"Great Political Wit,"* I got to see myself on the *Late Show*. I was on the book cover!

The Washington Post

LEADER DOLE HOSTS BARK BALL

When The Washington Humane Society asked me to be Chairdog of their annual Bark Ball in 1995, we all said BOW WOW! After all, it was through their kindness and care that I was adopted.

The Bark Ball is Washington's only formal evening for the four-on-the-floor crowd. It's every dog's chance to show off, wearing everything from denim and lace to pearls and diamonds. Dress is optional, so a few, like Ali the boxer, showed up in their birthday suits.

Bob and Elizabeth Dole's dog, Leader, is the honorary chairdog of this year's Bark Ball, the annual gala for the Washington Humane Society. The benefit takes place June 3, at the Loews L'Enfant Plaza Hotel.
© 1995 The Washington Post
Reprinted with permission

The highlight is always a huge silent auction, and according to advance notices about the 1999 Bark Ball, one item being offered was "brunch with Bob Dole". MMMM! I was definitely looking forward to that!

The best part about the Bark Ball? No cats allowed!

Washington Humane Society
BARK BALL
TOP HATS & TAILS

Mr. September

I literally jumped at every chance to help the Humane Society. When Ralston Purina asked me to be Mr. September for their 1998 Calendar and offered me $5,000, I said "YES!" and told Elizabeth and Bob "to give the check to the Washington Humane Society."

The Washington Post
Friday, May 2 1997

The Reliable Source
By Ann Gerhart and Annie Groer

NOW YOU KNOW...

Shortly after he lost his '96 White House run, Bob Dole made ads for Air France and Visa. Now his schnauzer, Leader is set to appear in a dog food calendar.

"Despite the election results, Leader is still top dog." Dole said yesterday of his 14-year-old pooch. Leader's $5,000 fee from the Purina Calendar of Champions will be donated to the Washington Humane Society, where Elizabeth Dole adopted the dog for her husband.

© 1997 The Washington Post
Reprinted with permission

Presentation of my $5,000 check to the Washington Humane Society.

Left to right: Claude Alexander, Executive Director, Ralston Purina; Elizabeth, Bob, Mary Healey, Executive Director, Humane Society; Susan Bury, President, Humane Society

September

Bring out the Champion in your dog.

Leader
Miniature Schnauzer

"Leader was a surprise gift from my wife, Elizabeth, after I was first elected Senate Majority Leader in 1984, and he's been a loyal friend ever since. He comes to the office with me every day, and in 1996, Leader campaigned tirelessly for the canine vote!"

Bob Dole
Former Senate Majority Leader & 1996 Republican Presidential Candidate

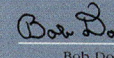

PET TIP

Take off on a brisk walk with your dog, and you'll both get the kind of high-energy exercise that benefits your cardiovascular system and helps control weight. Your dog will not only serve as a welcome companion, but he'll provide protection, too. Allow your dog to rest when he needs to, and provide only small amounts of water before, during and directly after exercise.

SUNDAY	MONDAY	TUESDAY	WEDNESDAY	THURSDAY	FRIDAY	SATURDAY
AUGUST	OCTOBER	1	2	3	4	5
6	7	8	9	10	11	12
	Labor Day					
13	14	15	16	17	18	19
20	21	22	23	24	25	26
	Rosh Hashanah begins at sundown					
27	28	29	30			
		Yom Kippur begins at sundown				

Willard Scott, a Horse and Me

I'll never forget an outdoor event in 1985 held on the Washington Monument grounds near the White House.

The plan was for NBC Weatherman Willard Scott to interview Elizabeth about a new transportation safety device. Of course, he wanted me to be on the show. This was to be my "big break" into network television. Being well connected, Willard had arranged perfect weather: a clear, warm, sunny spring day.

Everyone was rehearsed as to where they were to stand and in what order each would speak. Willard said this was live television and *nothing* could go wrong.

Just two minutes before we were to go on the air, a police officer riding a horse came over to see what was going on.

When I saw that horse come toward us, all heck broke loose. There was no way that horse was going to up-stage me. Neither the size of the horse nor the size of the rider gave me pause.

42

I broke out into the loudest barking tantrum you ever heard and nothing or no one could stop me. I was jumping and barking all at the same time, sometimes with all four feet off the ground. Willard was frantic, this was NOT what he had in mind and he immediately ordered my swift removal, I'm sure he feared for the safety of the horse.

Being the jovial genius that he is, Willard later forgave me for disrupting his show when I tried to pick a fight with that horse. Our paths crossed many times after that, but he never once brought it up; it was I who finally apologized when we shared this podium in 1998.

Kicking and barking, I was scooped up and carried away, out of sight and out of sound, and feeling very sad that I missed out on the chance of a lifetime. But I had no one to blame but myself.

Elated, Willard called a press conference; he officially accepted my apology and gave me a nice pat on the back. However, he balked when I suggested, "Let's kiss and make up!"

Elizabeth was so happy and proud of my reconciliation with Willard that she too came over and gave me a pat on the back.

43

Over Qualified?

My khaki trench coat was "just right" for my meeting with General Hugh Shelton, Chairman of the Joint Chiefs of Staff, and General Barry McCaffrey, Drug Enforcement Administrator.

Always on the lookout for a challenge, I asked about any openings for an experienced trooper such as myself. My several years of security work, combined with all I had learned just watching the K-9 Dogs with the Capitol Police, impressed them tremendously.

However, after study-

General Hugh Shelton
Chairman, Joint Chiefs of Staff

ing my demeanor and resume, they both came to the same conclusion: I was over-qualified. They suggested I try the CIA.

General (Ret.) Barry McCaffrey
Drug Czar

44

*Playing on the Capitol Lawn was a tough job,
but someone had to do it.*

My Hometown

Commuting to Capitol Hill along Constitution Avenue gave me a chance to relax and enjoy the sights of Washington. Security in the car was Wilbert's responsibility, so I stayed out of his way, unless he needed help. Weather permitting, I would rest my head on the window ledge to feel the breeze and to get a closer view. Realizing that I was now almost indispensable at both office and home, and concerned about my safety, Bob discouraged me from

While "Highest Office in the Land" refers to the President of the United States, for the citizens of Washington, D.C., our city's highest office holder is Mayor Anthony Williams.

He was glad to hear about my tour of Washington and took note that it had never been done by a dog before.

hanging my head out the window. He suggested instead that I take a nap, which I often did, especially in traffic jams.

Almost from the beginning, I noticed that all the people visiting Washington – the tourists – looked like they were having the time of their lives. People socialized with one another -- even with total strangers -- as they waited in long lines to see the White House. Kids were jumping and pointing at the big cement elephant at the Smithsonian where, nearby, a carousel was filled with children and grown ups happily riding the musical horses.

On a windy day, kites were flying around the Washington Monument. Near the Jefferson Memorial, couples would rent blue paddle boats to explore the Tidal Basin.

The tourists all share one characteristic: they all liked to have their picture taken in front of the monuments.

In 1996, photographer Lynn Dykstra took me to all these famous attractions and recorded the visits for my web site page, "Leader Tours Washington, D.C."

The monument photographs are arranged from East to West, beginning at Cedar Hill, the home of Frederick Douglass, and ending at the Lincoln Memorial.

One item every tourist needs is money, and they all want to see where the money is 'born'. Although I didn't get to see how it is made at the Bureau of Engraving, I liked the way they printed my picture on the $100 bill. When you visit you can do that, too.

47

Monumental Tour 1

Cedar Hill

Home of Frederick Douglass

"The best defense of free American institutions is the heart of the American people themselves"

Frederick Douglass

Plan to linger here. It's not easy to leave the cool breezes sweeping across this beautiful pastoral hilltop overlooking the city.

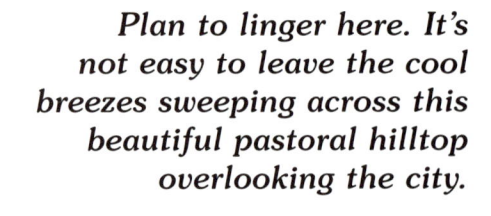

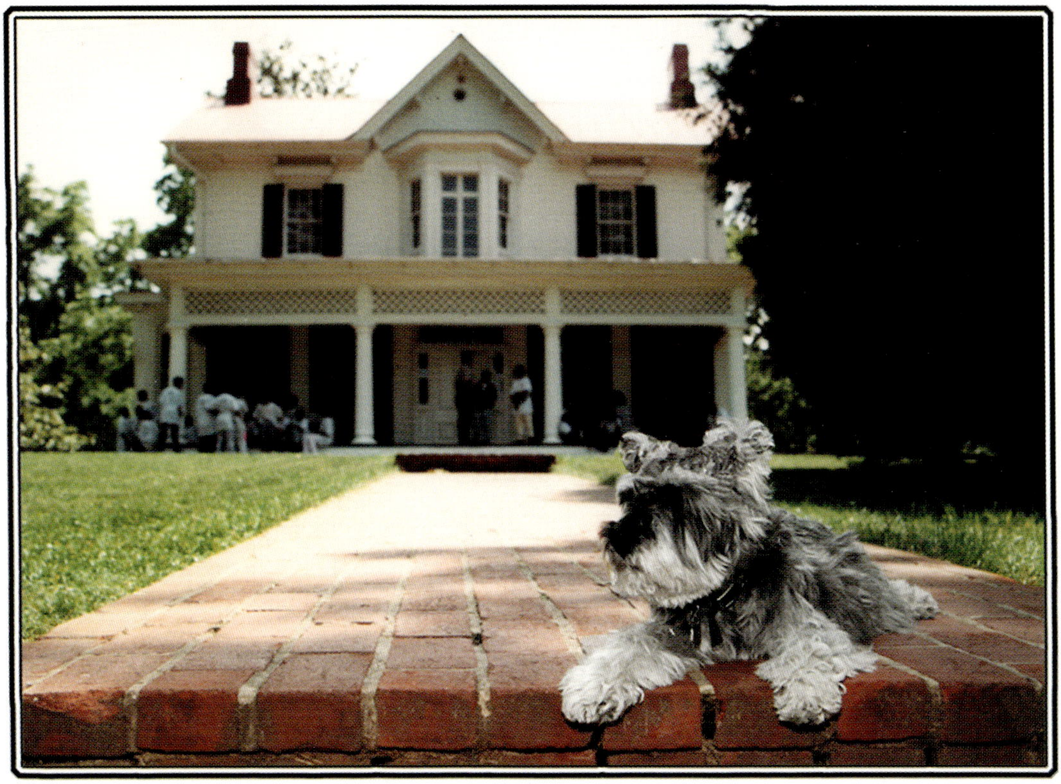

Monumental Tour 2

U.S. Capitol

Cradle of World Democracy

In this national stadium the big teams contend, not for a single afternoon but throughout the year.

My home away from home.

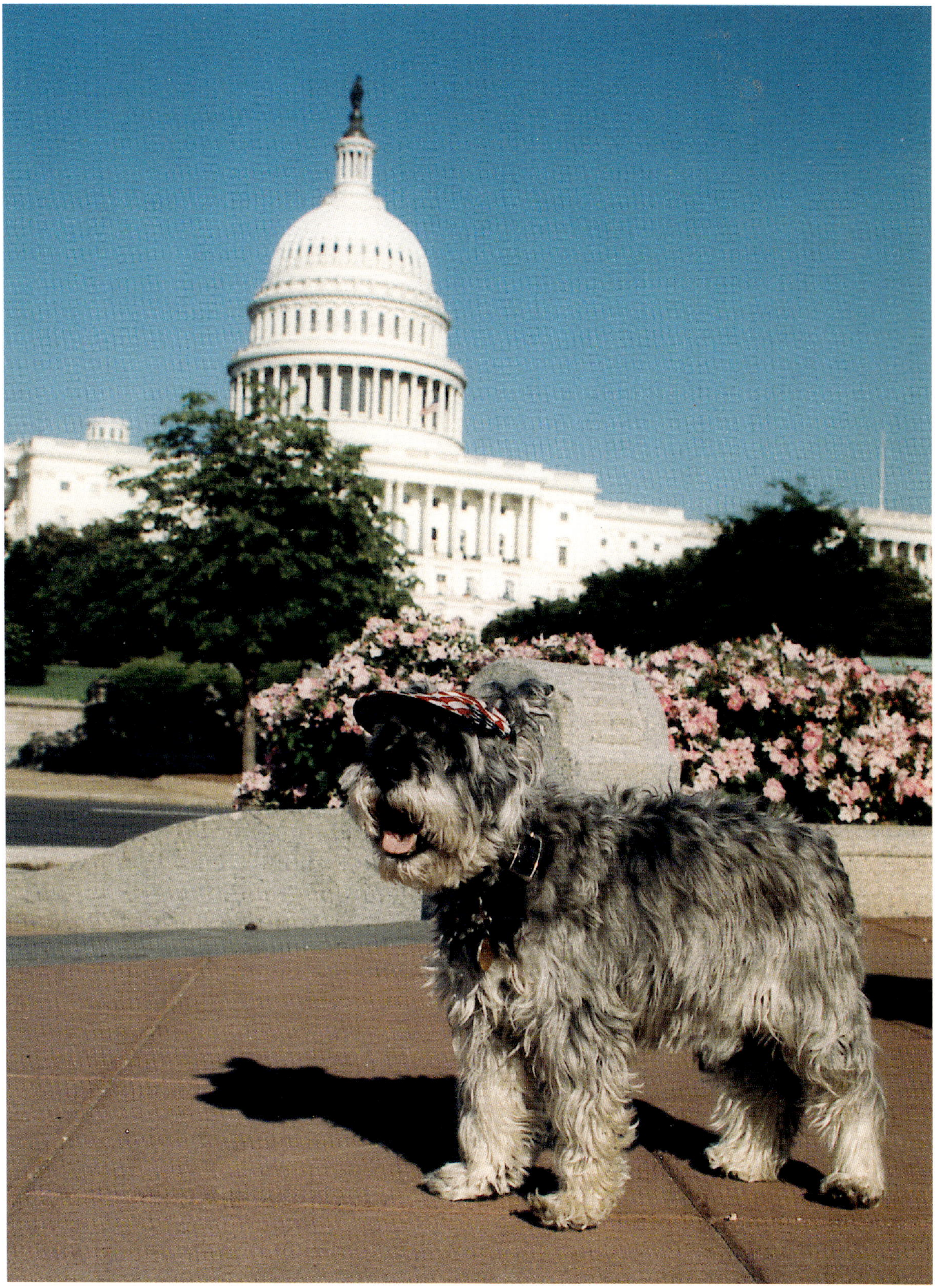

Monumental Tour 3

Smithsonian Institution
America's Attic

Jolly good of the Englishman James Smithson, who never visited the USA, to provide funds in his will to start this wonderful museum.

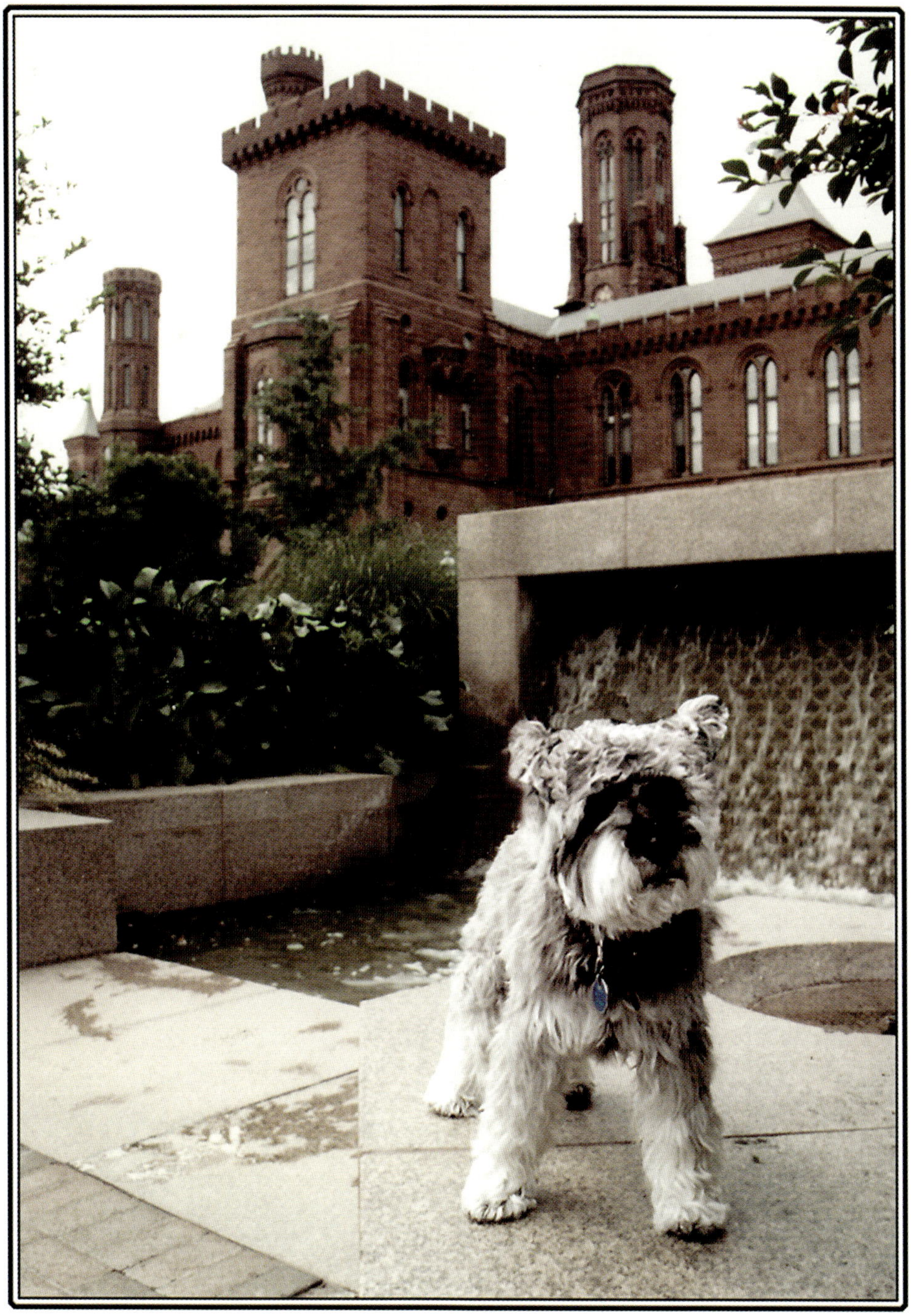

Monumental Tour 4

East Potomac Park

This 329 acre tract on the Potomac is shaped like a water-bird's head. Here you will find a 36-hole golf course, the Washington Rose Garden, and hundreds of double-blossom cherry trees.

This beautiful city park is located where George Washington reportedly tossed a coin across the Potomac.

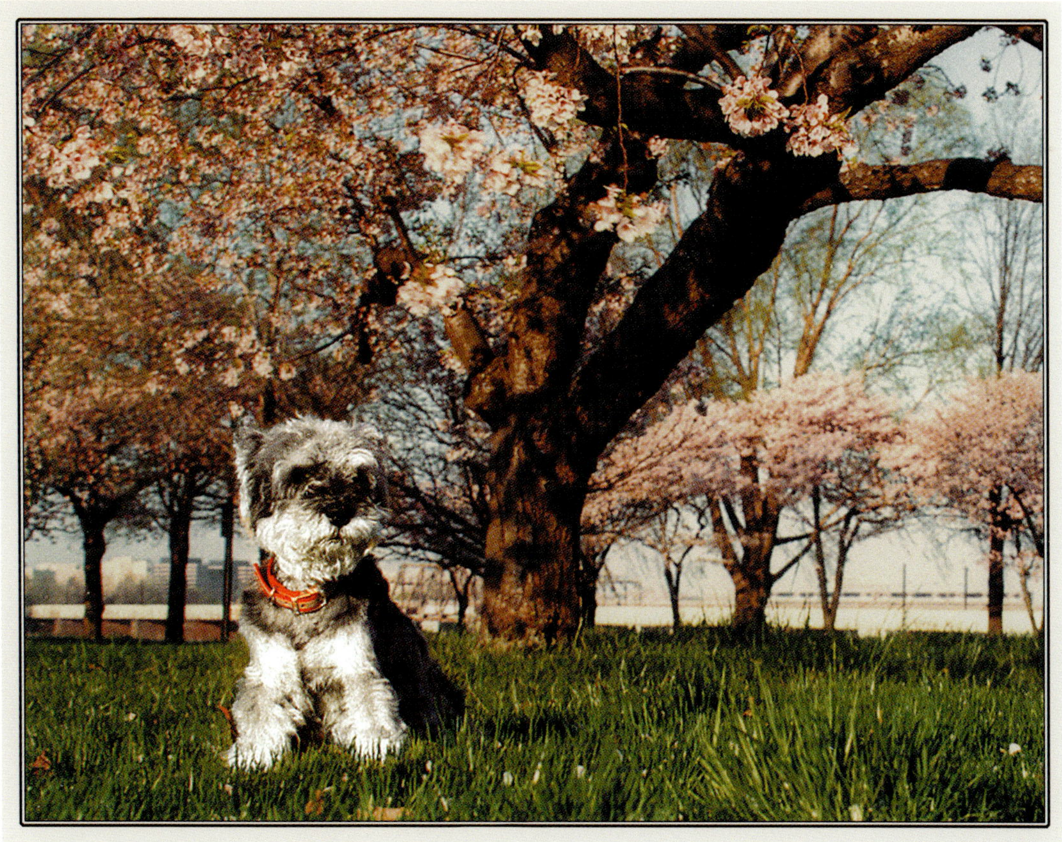

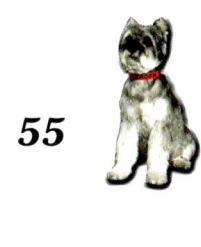

Monumental Tour 5

Jefferson Memorial
The Architect of our Liberty

My friends—the fish, the fowl and even the beaver, all live in these waters, and I know exactly where to find them.

56

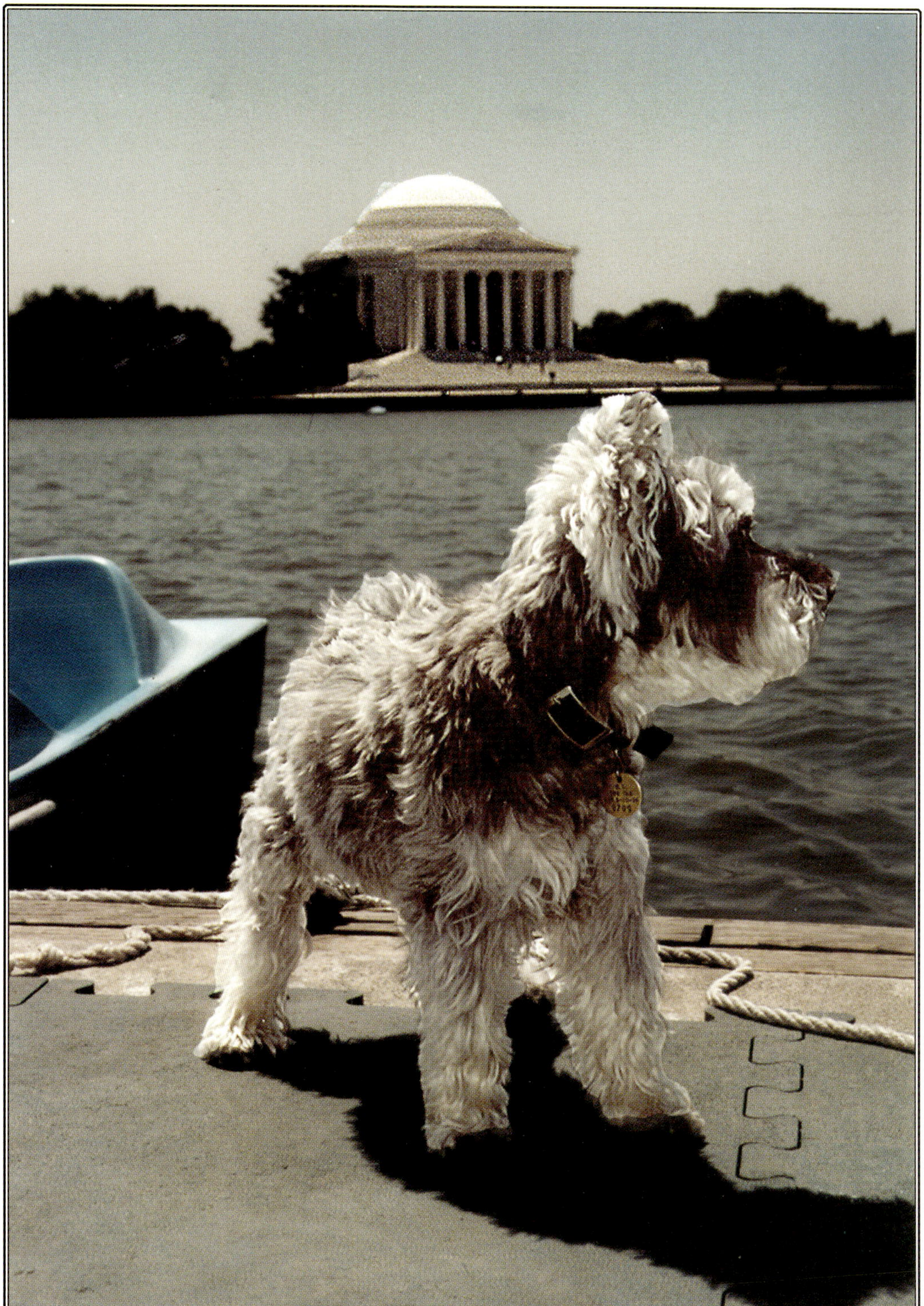

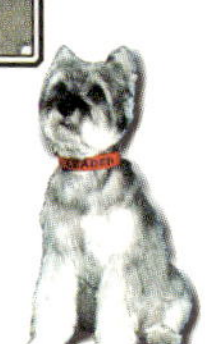

Monumental Tour 6

Washington Monument

"First in war, first in peace, first in the hearts of his countrymen"
Henry "Lighthorse" Lee, 1799

You'll find me here on the 4th of July, for music and magic. Those fireworks rattle my bones, but every year I come back for more.

59

Monumental Tour 7

Roosevelt Memorial

"I think I have a right to object to libelous statements about my dog Fala..."
FDR

Remember Fala? He lifted our hearts through some of our darkest hours. I often come here to sit by his side

HO) SEEK TO ESTABLISH
MS OF GOVERNMENT BASED ON
REGIMENTATION OF ALL HUMAN
S BY A HANDFUL OF INDIVIDUAL
ERS... CALL THIS A NEW ORDER.
NOT NEW AND IT IS NOT ORDER.

Monumental Tour 8

The White House

World's Most Famous Residence

"Washington is a city of southern efficiency and northern charm"

President John F. Kennedy, 1961

Home Sweet Home—almost! I did what I could, and beat Socks in the Internet Paw Poll.

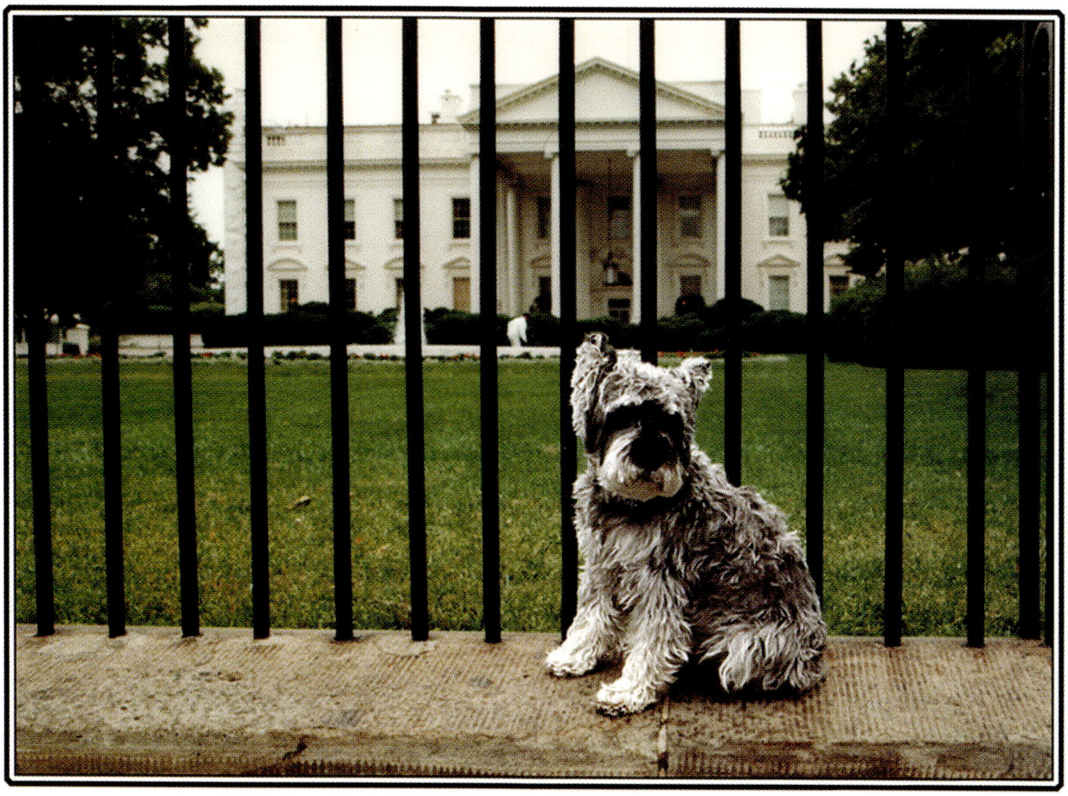

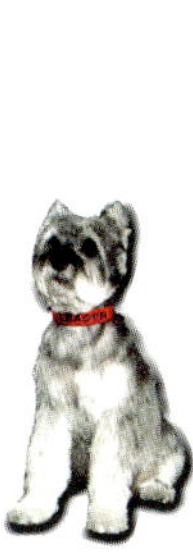

Monumental Tour 9

Lafayette Park

General Andrew 'Old Hickory' Jackson

Dedicated in 1853, this was the first equestrian statue in the United States.

Now that's how I like to find my horses—cast in bronze!

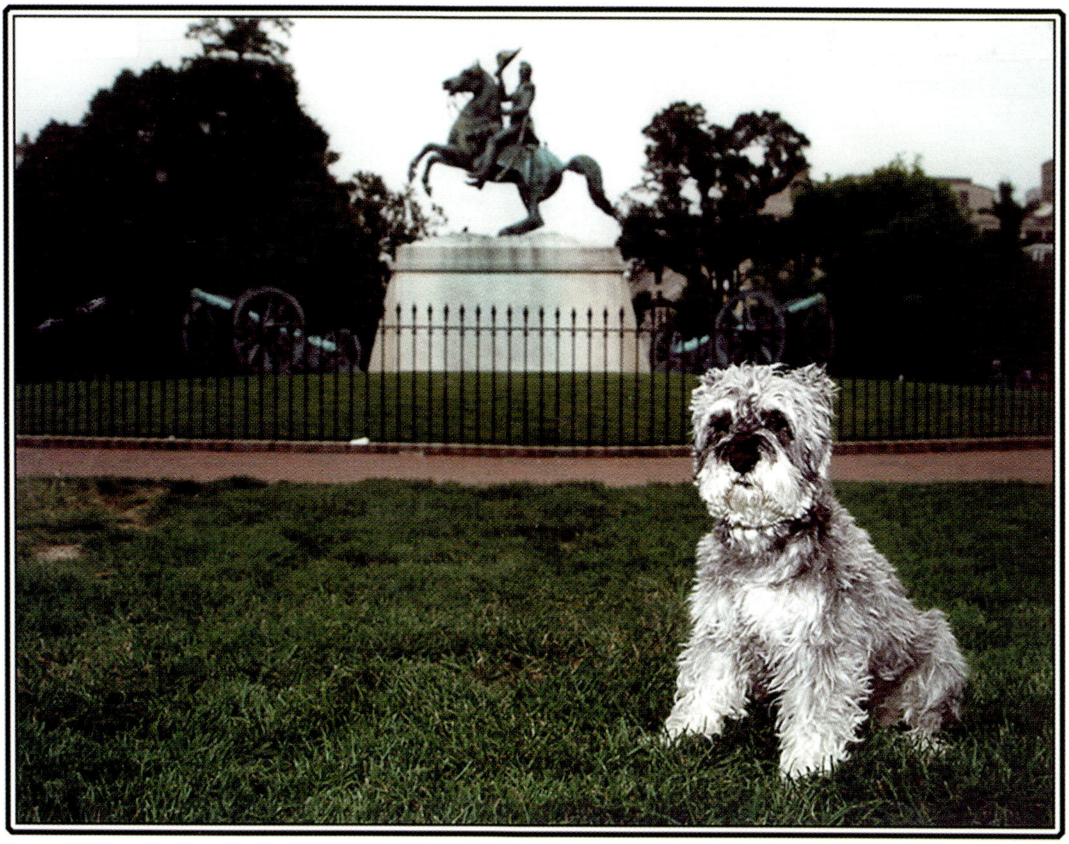

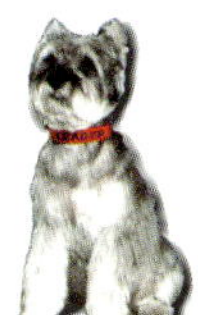

Monumental Tour 10

Simon Bolivar

His was a riches to rags story: born wealthy and aristocratic, he died penniless, having spent his entire fortune financing the liberation of South America from Spanish rule.

If I were a chihuahua, I could bark, Si! Si! Simon. This statue is in front of the Interior Department. We passed it every day on our way home.

LIBERATED VENEZUELA COLOMBIA ECUADOR PERU BOLIVIA AND PANAMA

Monumental Tour 11

West Potomac Park

Cherry Blossoms on the River Bank

It's all here! Take a walk on the mild side, watch the boat races, rest on a park bench, or just sit for hours and meditate under these Japanese cherry trees.

If you suffer from Potomac Fever (too much power), this is the ideal place to recuperate. There is nothing like a towering tree to bring you down to size.

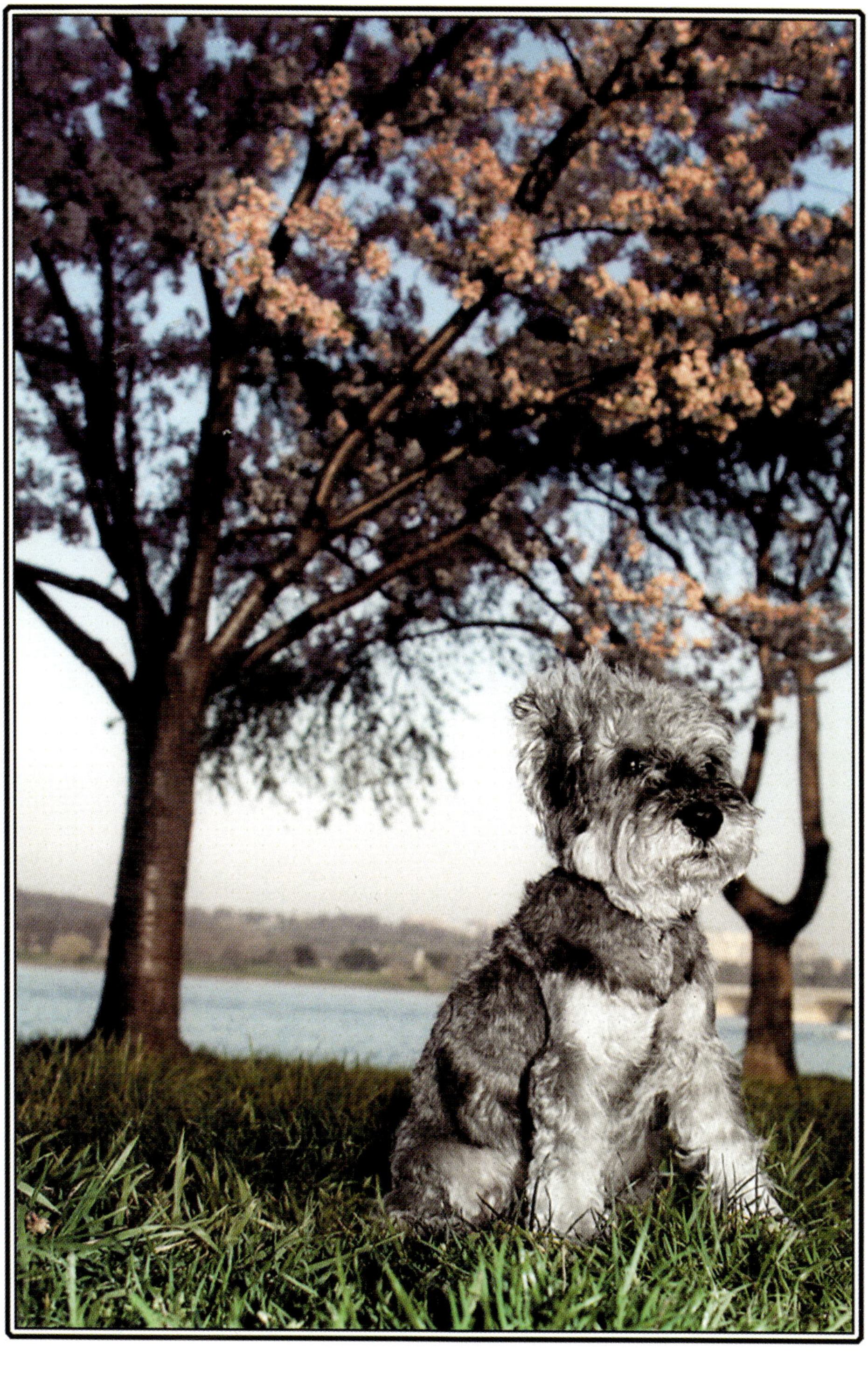

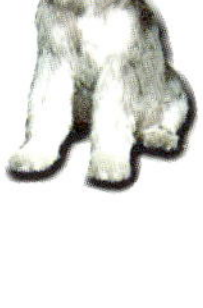

Monumental Tour 12

Vietnam Memorial

Maya Lin designed the v-shaped black granite wall inscribed with the names of 58,133 Americans who died or were missing in the Vietnam War.

Fallen Heroes

EDGAR LEE
LINWOOD R CUMBO
DONALD K McLEAN
JOHN A PROMBO
KENNETH E ROBERTS
DARREL T SWANSON
WALTER R TYRRELL
JAMES C BROWN
GEORGE J CANAMARE
FRED R FRAZIER Jr
ANDREW PEREZ GARCIA
CHRISTOPHER S SMITH
RODGER D HOWARD
PERRY D JOHNSON
DONALD L KIPP
ARTHUR L KLAUS
JAMES B McKNIGHT
STEVEN H NIPP
HENRY L PALMER
BRADFORD P SAWYER
JACK E SCHULTZ
RICHARD L SKOUBY
MICHAEL J SPEAR
RUSSELL B ADAMS
CLAUDE E BRAGG
MICHAEL T DECKER
JOE EDD HESTER
ROGER A MEYERS
GEORGE MEERDINK Jr
DONALD E PAXTON
ROBERT W TOPHAM Jr
ALONZO W WIGHT
GUY F ABBOTT
HOWARD ATKINSON
ANDREW J BELFIELD
THOMAS M BROWN
BILL D CALLAHAN
CHRISTOPHER CASIAS

Monumental Tour 13

The Reflecting Pool

This beautiful reflecting pool, linking the Washington Monument and the Lincoln Memorial, attracts geese, ice skaters, waders and Hollywood movie makers.

Here I 'reflect' on my campaign for First Dog.

73

Monumental Tour 14

Einstein Memorial

*"Politics is for the moment,
an equation is for eternity."*
Albert Einstein, 1934

Like many younger tourists,
I couldn't resist sitting on
Einstein's knee and contemplating
his concept of the universe.

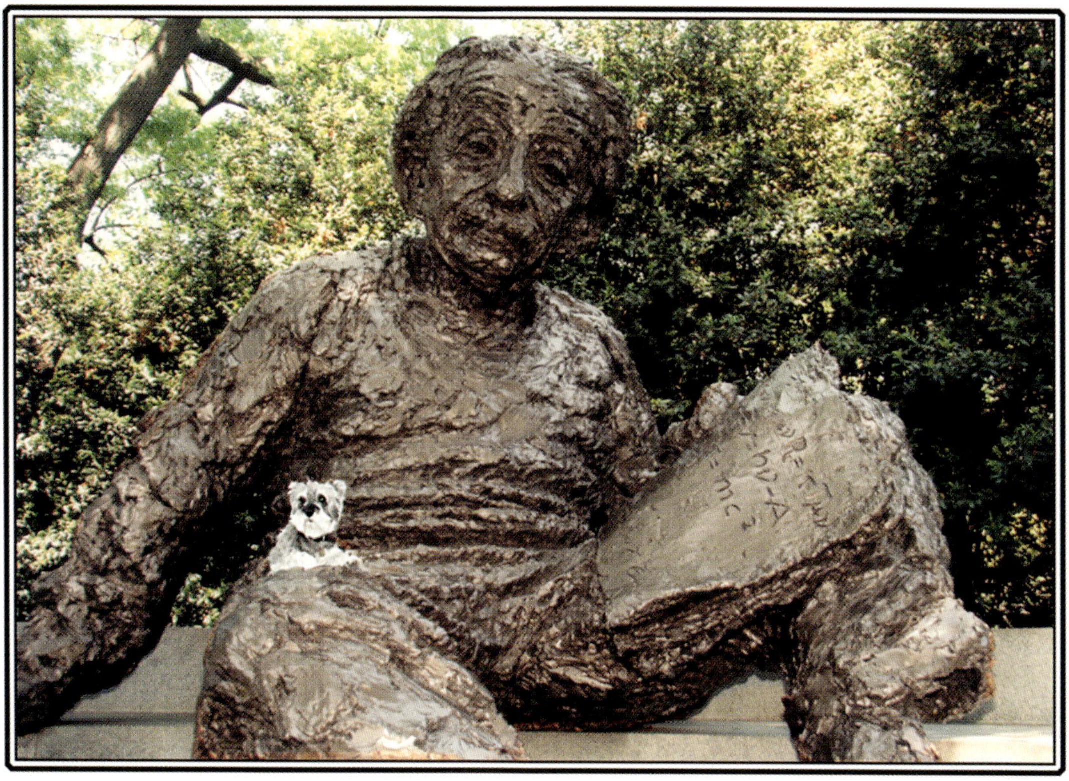

Monumental Tour 15

Lincoln Memorial

"Not often does a man arrive on earth who is both steel and velvet...as hard as rock and soft as velvet fog, who holds in his heart and mind the paradox of terrible storm and peace unspeakable."

Carl Sandburg

This is my favorite monument. Here I face a man who could have turned his back on enslaved men and women. But he did not.

With this, my whirlwind tour of the monuments concludes. To see my own contributions to America's political history, turn the page.

76

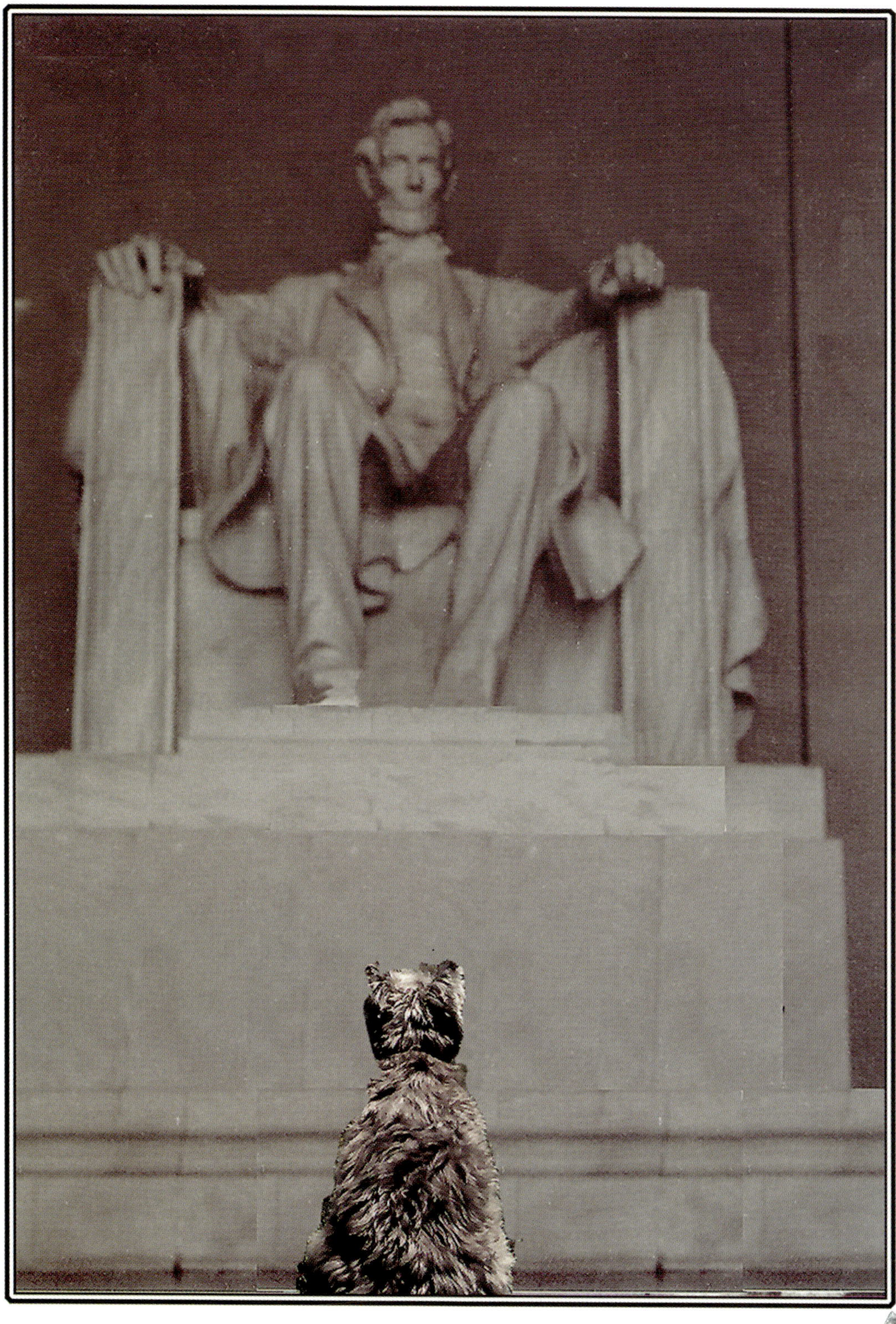

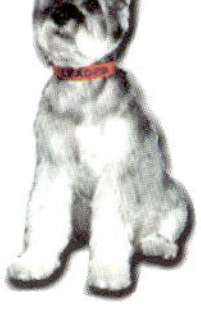

My Internet Victory!

The 1996 Presidential Paw Poll — FINAL RESULTS

EXTRA — Leader Wins!

as of November 5, 1996 at 5:01:38PM

LEADER 55.2 paw-cent

SOCKS 44.8 paw-cent

Robyn Frankel
Robyn Frankel Public Relations
for a client

www.firstdog.com

The '96 presidential primaries were coming up and, although he had not yet formally announced, Bob had long been referred to as the front runner.

Our respite from the public-eye was suddenly interrupted when my computer friends learned that Socks had a Home Page on the Internet. As expected, they declared: "If Socks has a Home Page, then Leader should have a Home Page!" Period.

Bob was not yet a candidate, but that didn't stop me from gearing up just in case.

First, I needed a web site domain. We decided on firstdog.com from Network Solutions. Webmaster Ted Christensen upgraded his Power Mac, ordered Page Mill, PowerPoint, a color scanner and a faster modem.

When Bob announced his candidacy for President on April 10, 1995, we were all set to go.

If elected First Dog, my promise was to "work night and day, except for naps, to show the world that I am more than just a furry face." Our slogan "Put a Leader in the White House" started appearing on badges, buttons and T-shirts.

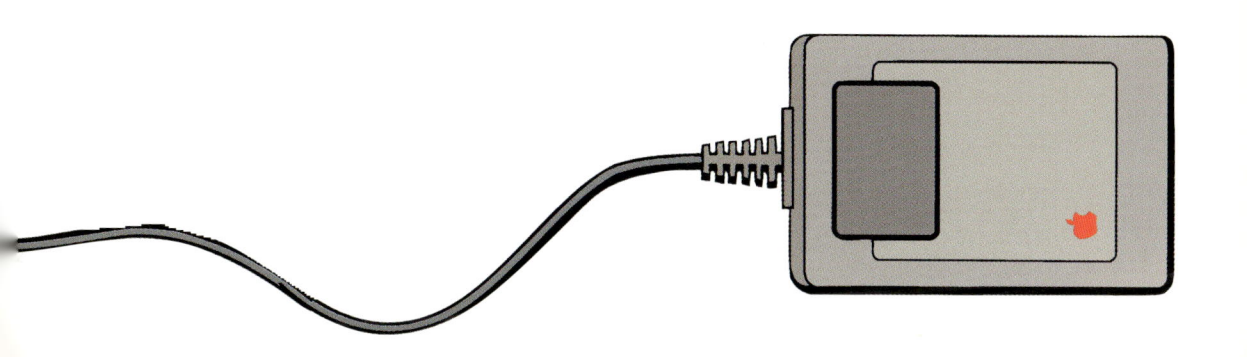

Welcome to Leader Dole's Home Page

LEADER DOLE FIRST DOG 96

Put a Leader in the White House

The Story of Leader Dole

This is the story of a minature schnauzer named Leader. At the age of 2, Leader was adopted from a Washington DC animal shelter by a lovely couple in search of a pet. ... (Click for more)

Click Here — INTERNET FRIENDS

Leader Tours Washington DC — Click Here

LEADER'S T-SHIRTS and BUTTONS — CLICK HERE

BOB DOLE 1996 — ELECT THE MAN FROM RUSSELL KANSAS

Official Dole Campaign Home Page

Click Here

Endorsements poured in. The very first one came from Sniffer Batt, the First Dog of Idaho. Soon, other members of the animal kingdom jumped on my bandwagon. We posted many of the photographs and letters as they came in: Cliff, the Pennsylvania iguana; Khemosabey, a horse from Delaware; Boom, our three-legged dog from Ohio, to mention just a few.

When I received Sniffer's pictures and letter of support, I was on cloud nine; many other First Dogs from states across the nation followed. A special one came from Spot Bush, the First Dog of Texas. I had known Spot's mother, Millie Bush, when she was in the White House and I was in the Senate. In her best seller, "Millie's Book," she printed my Press Release vigorously defending her against the WASHINGTONIAN magazine's defamatory article declaring her "Washington's Ugliest Dog."

NEWS From the

LEADER

(R-Kansas) SH 141 Hart Building, Washington, D.C. 20510-1601

FOR IMMEDIATE RELEASE   CONTACT: WALT RIKER
THURSDAY, JUNE 29, 1989   (202) 224-5358

LEADER: WASHINGTONIAN ATTACK ON FIRST DOG MILLIE
AN "ARF"FRONT TO DOGS EVERYWHERE

WASHINGTON -- CALLING IT AN "ARF"FRONT TO DOGS EVERYWHERE, "LEADER," FIRST K-9 ASSISTANT TO SENATE REPUBLICAN LEADER BOB DOLE (R-KS.) SAID TODAY THAT WASHINGTONIAN MAGAZINE WAS "BARKING UP THE WRONG FIRE HYDRANT" WHEN IT PICKED FIRST DOG "MILLIE" AS WASHINGTON'S UGLIEST DOG IN ITS CURRENT "BEST & WORST" LIST.

"I TALKED WITH MILLIE ABOUT THIS TODAY," LEADER SAID, "I ADVISED HER TO HAVE PUPPIES."

Leader's Friends and Supporters

Leader Dole First Dog '96

SNIFFER BATT
Firstdog of Idaho

BRIG with Samuel
(Sen. Slade Gorton's grandson)

PUDGE
with Sen. Larry Craig

RAINBOW
Mississippi Gov. Kirk Fordice

GUS with Senator Phil Gramm

ALLIE & MOLLIE RIDGE
Gov. & Mrs. Tom Ridge of Pennsylvania

BOOM from OHIO

DAVID with JUDGE
David is the son of Gov. & Mrs.
David M. Beasley of South Carolina

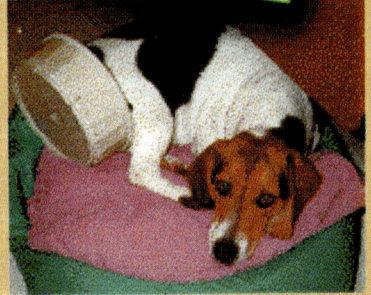

MARIA from Arizona

The POWER of the Press

When THE WASHINGTON POST, always on the lookout for a super scoop, heard about my home page, they featured their "find" with this article. Wire services picked up

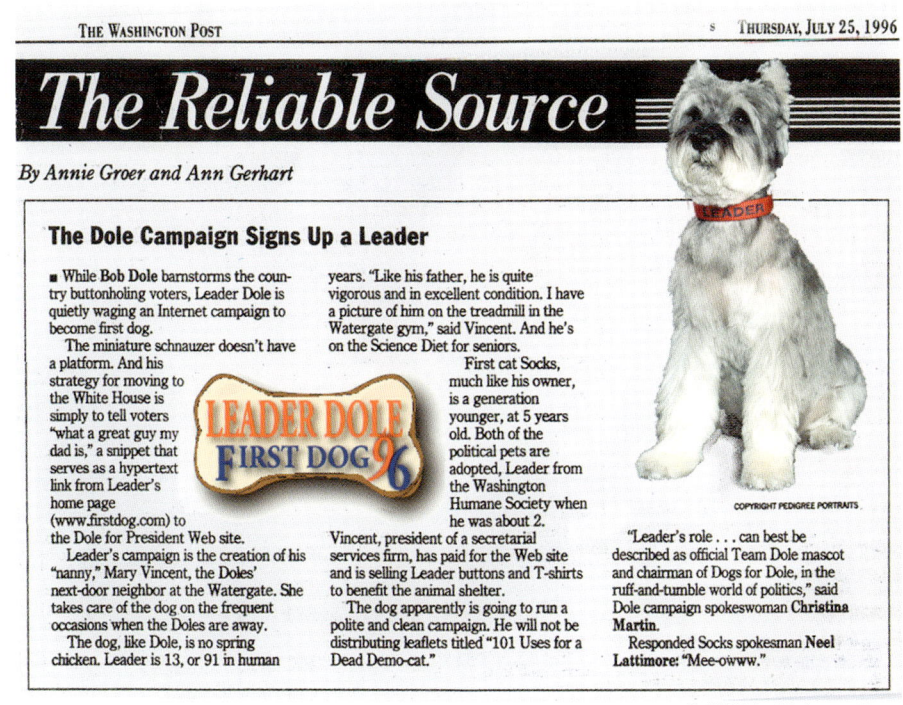

THE WASHINGTON POST — **THURSDAY, JULY 25, 1996**

The Reliable Source

By Annie Groer and Ann Gerhart

The Dole Campaign Signs Up a Leader

■ While Bob Dole barnstorms the country buttonholing voters, Leader Dole is quietly waging an Internet campaign to become first dog.

The miniature schnauzer doesn't have a platform. And his strategy for moving to the White House is simply to tell voters "what a great guy my dad is," a snippet that serves as a hypertext link from Leader's home page (www.firstdog.com) to the Dole for President Web site.

Leader's campaign is the creation of his "nanny," Mary Vincent, the Doles' next-door neighbor at the Watergate. She takes care of the dog on the frequent occasions when the Doles are away.

The dog, like Dole, is no spring chicken. Leader is 13, or 91 in human years. "Like his father, he is quite vigorous and in excellent condition. I have a picture of him on the treadmill in the Watergate gym," said Vincent. And he's on the Science Diet for seniors.

First cat Socks, much like his owner, is a generation younger, at 5 years old. Both of the political pets are adopted, Leader from the Washington Humane Society when he was about 2.

Vincent, president of a secretarial services firm, has paid for the Web site and is selling Leader buttons and T-shirts to benefit the animal shelter.

The dog apparently is going to run a polite and clean campaign. He will not be distributing leaflets titled "101 Uses for a Dead Demo-cat."

"Leader's role . . . can best be described as official Team Dole mascot and chairman of Dogs for Dole, in the ruff-and-tumble world of politics," said Dole campaign spokeswoman **Christina Martin**.

Responded Socks spokesman **Neel Lattimore**: "Mee-owww."

© 1996 The Washington Post
Reprinted with permission

the story, and it was reprinted in other newspapers around the world. Since it carried my Internet address, I was deluged with e-mail, which made me realize how lucky I was to have the Internet to broadcast our message.

Internet Paw Poll Launched

CPI Corp. of St Louis joined the excitement with their Presidential Paw Poll between Socks and Leader. You know what the result was; and I'd like to show you how I beat the famous feline. Socks was ahead when the Paw Poll was first posted but it didn't take me long to catch up and

83

Leader's Friends and Supporters

LEADER DOLE FIRST DOG '96

MR. T from Alexandria Virginia

CLIFF from Pennsylvania

LUCKY BOY
Sacramento California

OTTO from Virginia

ELLA from West Virginia

BUNGEE and Friend
North Carolina

Carol holding ANNIE
Ohio

CORKY from Georgia

MAGGIE from California

KHEMOSABEY from Delaware

stay ahead. I placed a handy voting button on my homepage, and articles like this one generated a lot of votes.

The Internet Times

First nationwide presidential 'paw poll'

The race is "neck and neck" in the first-ever nationwide "Paw Poll" to determine voters' choice for "First Pet". The Democrat's "Socks," Clinton's black-and-white mixed cat, is just a whisker ahead of the Republican's "Leader," Dole's grayish-black schnauzer —50.1 percent to 49.9 percent, as of last week.

While President Bill Clinton and Bob Dole continue to pander to the public, their respective pets are appealing to voters purely on the basis of "paw-litical" preferences. The "paw-litical" candidates' campaign slogans are identical: "Vote and vote often."

The presidential "Paw Poll" began Aug. 6 and continues through the November election on the strictly "non-pawtisan" home pages of CPI Photo/Fox Photo at http://www.cpiphoto.com and http://www.foxphoto.com.

Unlike other polls, results of the 1996 Presidential Paw Poll are updated every ten minutes. Voters of any age may participate, there's no limit on the number of times you can vote, and there's no electoral college.

U.S. NEWSWIRE

Jonathan Karl, CNN, was covering political campaign spots, so I faxed him a note about my home page and the Paw Poll. He e-mailed me back, saying he liked the page but could not find Socks' home page. I told him Socks didn't have a home page of his own but only shared the official White House site.

The kids edition of TIME magazine inquired about my site and featured my story and a picture on their cover.

TIME FOR KIDS
WHO'S NEWS — ELECTION

A New Leader

Will **LEADER** replace Socks as First Pet? Bob Dole's miniature schnauzer loved running around Washington with Dole, and still likes to play guard dog for the candidate. Elizabeth Dole gave the pup to her husband more than 10 years ago. When the election heated up, Leader took it easy. He mostly snoozed in Mrs. Dole's office at campaign headquarters.

85

Leader's Friends and Supporters

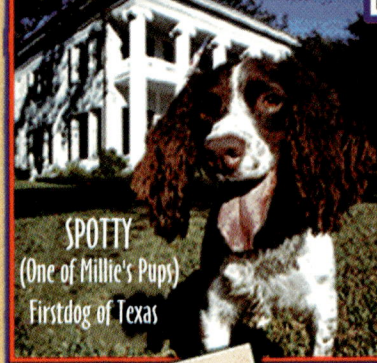

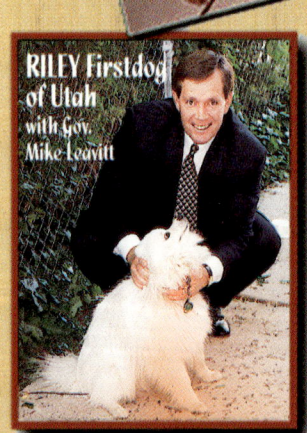

LEADER DOLE FIRST DOG 96

ROSIE WELD — Firstdog of Massachusetts

MARIA from Maryland

SUGAR COATS — Owner of Sen. Dan Coats

MISS TAYLOR from OHIO

SHAYNA From Dale City Virginia

ALVIN from Florida

SPOTTY (One of Millie's Pups) Firstdog of Texas

Ralph, Arwen, Beaureard, Jake & Bubkis from Vine Grove Kentucky

HEIDI BEAR Florida

RILEY Firstdog of Utah with Gov. Mike Leavitt

Jefferson Pataki Firstdog of New York

MAGNUM GR with Indiana Senator & Mrs. Lugar

A Peeping TOM?

I asked my web master to check the site-logs daily to see who was looking at my home page. We were surprised to see that someone in the White House had looked in several times! There was only one prime suspect with a well known addiction to nocturnal excursions and general nosiness: Socks, the peeping tom! We were simply amused and never let it be known that we were aware of his identity.

Further investigation of Socks had to wait, as I was busy being interviewed by PEOPLE magazine for an article that gave my site even more national exposure. We were on a roll!

■ TAKE ME TO YOUR LEADER

In the dog-eat-dog world of presidential races, the Web is the hot campaign tool. So Mary Vincent—Bob Dole's neighbor at Washington's Watergate apartments and dogsitter to his miniature schnauzer Leader—launched First Dog (http://www.first-dog.com), where the 13-year-old fluffball is shown in front of capital landmarks. Other GOP pols, including Phil Gramm and George W. Bush, have also sent in pooch photos. Says Vincent, who'll donate button and T-shirt profits to the local Humane Society, Leader's former home: "When you see pets, you forget politics." ■ LAURA SMITH KAY

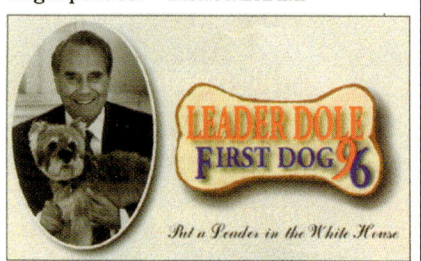

▲ You can pick a bone with Bob Dole's schnauzer on a need-to-gnaw basis.

Reprinted from the Sept. 9, 1996 issue of PEOPLE weekly magazine by special permission, ©1996, Time Inc.

87

Leader's Friends and Supporters

CHARLIE BEAR

LIEBER
East Rockaway, New York

BOOM AGAIN !
with 'new' Mom in Athens Ohio

TAR II

MISTY
Fairfax, Virginia

KALI & MAX

Leader's
Official Mail Bag

OFFICE OF THE GOVERNOR
P.O. BOX 83720
BOISE 83720-0034

PHILIP E. BATT
GOVERNOR

(208) 334-2100

May 21, 1996

Leader Dole for First Dog
1996 Campaign Headquarters
2818 Pennsylvania Avenue, N.W.
Washington, D.C. 20007

Dear Leader,

    Thank you for asking me to join you in Cyberspace. I am pleased to accept your invitation.

    I have enclosed a data sheet, a biography, and two colored photographs. In the first photo, I am hard at work in my office. Some people refer to this as the Governor's Office, but a few of us actually know who runs the show around here. In the second shot, I was approaching my assistant, Jacque, the First Lady of Idaho, to explain how to adjust the light to get my best side. Unfortunately, she went ahead and took the picture before I was ready.

    As you can see, there are many challenges in serving as a First Dog. However, I wish you the best of luck in your campaign. I am certain you will be a effective leader, Leader. Please let me know if I may be of further assistance. I'd be happy to do anything I can to help you knock the "socks" off that darned cat.

Loyally,

Sniffer Batt
First Dog

SB:bjs

Leader's bone-mail

Dear Mr. Leader:
You are my hero; you are the third coolest dog in America. The first is my dog and my friends dog in Mass. If you are a female, here is my address to my dog who is a male.

Please write back.
Sincerely,
Travis Brooks

7/12/96
I love the First Dog web page! Thanks telling me about it... although I couldn' find the link to the Socks home page..

Thanks!
Jonathan Karl
CNN

Hi Leader. My name is Mr. Tibbs. I am a Llhasso Apso. I used to be Tibby but my new foster parents changed it to Mr. Tibbs since I am a senior citizen (14yrs old). My daddy had to go into a nursing home and I adopted the man who used to deliver meals on wheels. I don't know what political party my daddy was but now I am a staunch republican. I hope you move into the white house in January. I'm not barking up the wrong tree either. Tell your mommy and daddy we all love them and think they are great.
Mr. Tibbs

Jim Messer 11/2/96 Re Senator Mitchell

Dear Leader,
Countless times I walked you from the Hart Office Building to your favorite haunts. Some of my favorite times were when you'd chew on Sen. Mitchell's shrubbery in front of his little blue house and that little lady would come outside and yell, "...and you tell Bob Dole to keep that dog tied up and away from this house."

Well good luck, little fella see you in January.
Ciao little fella.

Jim Messer
Hart Office Jan-July 1993

From: MGriff
To: leader@firstdog.com
Subject: CANADIAN GREETINGS!!!!

Just visited your "page" and really enjoyed it! Your friends in the north are following your progress closely.
We wish you well and LOVE your dog.

PHOEBE the Dachshund
BOW WOW!!
I am a very young pedigree Dachshund and I really enjoyed reading about you. I hope some day to visit the White House and this seems to be my best chance.
BOW WOW...
Phoebe

ROLLR - 9/5/96
ROCKIN'
This is the coolest site. It is too cool that a dog has his own website.
Leader is AWESOME!

9/18/96
HELLO FROM RIO
Hi Leader my name is Queenie and I live in Rio, Brazil. I'm hoping to see you running by the Oval Office next year! Do you like soccer?

Queenie

Svein F. Oftebro, 8/13/96
NORWAY
HEY!
Vaff! VOV!
voff aff a voff, Arf arrf piv voffaboff!
Don't you think?
LOVE from Vinnie, Kinko and all the other republican dogs in Norway!

Matt 10/18/96
GO LEADER!
GO BOB!
From 2 Republicans and 1 Miniature Schnauzer

Greetings from former First Dogs (Schnauzers)
Hi Leader,
Our names are Holly and Pepper Wilson. Our father was president of a homeowners association, so we thought your could benefit form some of our experience: (1) Never chase the vice president's cat. (2) Always have the pooper scooper when you go out for a walk, especially when you are on "common ground". (3) Only beg for treats at dessert time. Good Luck with your quest.
Bye for now.
Holly and Pepper (Wuff-Wuff).

11/1/96-Fourth Grade Class in Maize Kansas

Dear Leader,
Your home page was the first place our class visited on our newly connected internet computer. If you read this please bark back.

Thank you

Date: Sat, 13 Jul 1996
To: leader@firstdog.com
Subject: arf arf ruuuufffff

arf arf linked to your bark bark site.

Heard about it on arf arf CNN last bark bark night

David Jo, - Re: My Human
I am a 2-year-old cockatiel and my human likes and is going to vote for your human.
Hope to visit you in the big White House.
Plenty of space to fly around!!!
See you later Leader Dole
David

Date: Fri, 12 Jul 1996 22:40:00 -0500
To: leader@firstdog.com
Subject: From Mitzi

Woof,
I am 1' 3" tall Alabama girl!! I love to run around in the backyard, chase squirrels, warn my parents of strangers approaching and my favorite is my dads pot roast! Curious if we may meet one day!
Love
Mitzi

Karen Greenberg 10/7/96 LEADER'S TOUR
Dear Leader:
You are a very cute dog. I hope you had a nic time touring the city. It is my understanding that you have a good working knowledge of capital but that you would like to move up to the White House. Good Luck to you and yo owners; you look very plucky.
Kitty

8/18/96 Good Luck from Kansas Charlie
I saw a little piece in the Montreal paper about your home page and I decided to visit it -- it is GREAT - as a miniature schnauzer, I am very proud to see one of our own rise to such heights! My name is Charlie and I am a miniature schnauzer living here in Montreal! My full name is "Decscarino Kansas Charlie"-- the first name is of the kennel where my owners found me - Kansas is the state where one of my owners is from and Charlie is my name given to me by my other owner.
I wish you and your master all the best--good luck Leader Dole! Cheers from Montreal!
Charlie the Schnauzer

SCHNAUZER FOR FIRST DOG!
Leader,
Why didn't you get to go on the 96 hour tour? My owner always lets me fly with her, and yours has his own plane so you could fly up top instead of in cargo. I'm keeping my paws crossed that you get in the White House.
Kelly B. Hoover, Miniature Schnauzer par excellence

Cardinal Hill Imaging, 7/7/96
To Leader from the Gang
Hey Leader: In Pine Grove, Kentucky, we are all pulling for you. We were all also homeless or at the Harding County Anima Shelter. We are Jake (German Shepherd), Beauregard (Lab), Bubkis (mix?) Ralph (Cocker Spaniel) and Arwen (mix?). GOOD LUCK TO YOU AND YOUR HUMANS!

8/14/96
GREETINGS FROM NORWAY!
A masterpiece of a homepage.

If Senator Dole doesn't win the election with his dog on the net, I should be the first to declare the world officially insane.
GOOD LUCK
Audun Nordal
Norway

Chippy the Jack Russell Terrier
I am a two-year-old Jack Russell Terrier and even though I am too young to vote, I might be able to influence other dogs, including my brother Leroy a 7-year-old doberman. Best of Luck in your campaign.
Sincerely
Chippy Schmidt

GO LEADER in 1996!!
Dear Leader,
I am a Republican Boxer and I see your picture at Chichie's dog salon where I may have shared the bathtub next to yours. My family is voting to make you first dog. We're with you all the way.

Love
Valentina the Boxer

Leader's Home Page
Fun web site. I'll bet Fala would have had his own home page too!

Best Wishes
Al Williamson
Charlottesville, Virginia

SLZMQ, 10/23/96 Yo
You know, Mr. Firstdog (almost), it's gonna be a tough job being the First Dog. So if you ever need anyone to talk to, don't be afraid to give me a call. Just e-mail me and I'll be there. So I'm here for you. Later dude.
Chad R. Sorenson

BEST WISHES 7/27/96
I am a 2-year-old Bichon Frise who lives in Clarksburg, Md. with my parents. We all hope to see you in the White House. You are an inspiration to all us K-9s.
Sincerely
Buggsy

Date: Sta, 01 June 1996

Hi Leader:
I hope we will see you at the White House front-lawn very very soon.
All my best wishes for you and, of course, Bob Dole.
GOOD LUCK
from a friend from Germany!

Patrick

Re: White House
Hope to see your pretty face in the White House soon.

Sincerely,
Cheers

(German Shepherd dog - Ohio)

Date: Mon, 05, August 1996
From: Marianne Michelsen - FINLAND

Greetings from 2 black Finnish cocker spaniel! If it is possible to get a photo of You and Your master please send it to us.
Marianne Michaelsen

With special regards from:
Bertie and Humphrey

10/26/96 HI!

Please say Hello to me.
I have no life.

Sleepless in Columbus

Hi--I am a 3-year-old Sheltie in Dallas, TX who writes for our travel agency newsletter. Would love to have Leader Dole write a guest column in our October issue--just send it via e-mail.
Best of Luck in November
Little Mac

dearest Leader...
I dropped by your homepage in the internet and found you adorable...I am even interested in acquiring your T-shirt...however, because I live in Korea I was wondering whether the T-shirt was limited to those in the US only.
Thanks
Samui

Subject: T-shirt offer

I'd really love to add a link to my home-page, except I'm using the Vermont State Junior Jersey Club homepage (the little brown Borden cows). Although Vermont is historically a Republican state, I feel the Jr. Jersey page should remain non-partisan (although you are awfully cute).

Good Luck
Mary

HI LEADER....
Great pictures on the web, you are a good looking dog, you lucky dog!!!
Can't wait til you take over the White House.
Best Regards and keep up the good work.
--Ham Radio Operator W7US in Arizona.

SCHNAUZERS RULE!!
We are five Giant Schnauzers in Dallas, TX here. We surf for schnauzer stuff and found your page. We are voting for "Leader in the White House" and mom will too so that is six votes from Dallas.
Regards, Pistol, Hannaah, Libby, Jones and Harleigh...
and our mom, Debbie

Good Luck Leader;
Hope you get to the White House--good luck--I am a 7-year-old mini schnauzer, my mom got me as a birthday present...my whole family is going to be voting so you'll have your chance in the White House...got my paws crossed...Jiggs

7/29/96 - HI FROM AUSTRALIA!
Dearest Leader:
Hi my name is Jacco and I have two dogs who live here in Australia with me. Their names are Edge (she was named after the U2 guitarist) and Layla.
They would like to know what type of food the first dog has for breakfast. We wait in anticipation for your hasty reply.
Yours, Jaclyn, Edge amd Layla McDonald

Cyber Poet

My web site inspired this very clever poem e-mailed from Shotzie Foley, Fort Myers, Florida.

Subject: Greetings
From: Another Schnauzer

Dear Leader,

My Mom and my Dad
Were just surfing the Net
Your Home Page, they said
Was as good as they get.

They shared it with me
Cause I don't have a clue
I'm not only a dog
I'm a Schnauzer, like you.

They've taught me some tricks
I'll perform for a treat
A cookie - a bone
Or a small piece of meat.

I'll jump through a hoop
I'll sit or I'll beg
Roll over three times
Or I'll shake with my leg.

Shotzie Foley and Friend

But their favorite trick
Has political tones
The reaction is mixed
Some cheers - some groans.

Would you rather be Clinton
Or a really dead dog?
I fall on my back
Just as stiff as a log.

Four paws in the air
My choice is quite clear
The Democrats moan
The Republicans cheer !

Say Hi to your Mom
Good Luck to your Dad
He's got two votes here
and I'm sure he'll be glad.

If you're ever nearby
Just pick up the phone
And we'll both get together
And share a big bone.

I'll stop by the White House
If I'm in D.C.
Because after November
That's where you will be!

In addition to support for my campaign, my internet site also generated income for the Washington Humane Society, as orders for my official t-shirts and buttons kept coming in from as far away as Korea and Japan.

Official Campaign Kit

BEST FIRST PET DEBATE

The war between Socks and Leader might have been started on the Internet, but it soon spread to other battlefields. The Humane Society of the United States created a major media event with John McLaughlin moderating the

Fight for the run of the White House

By Carl Schoettler, *The Baltimore Sun*

■ **Debate:** *The puns fly a whole lot faster than the fur as tongue-in-cheek debate seeks the best pet for the top job.*

By Carl Schoettler
SUN STAFF

The great Presidential Pet Debate made cats and dogs sound so doggone good you could wonder why we bother putting people in the White House at all.

Nipping at the heels of the last Clinton-Dole debate, far livelier dog and cat lovers went at each other paw to claw, not to mention tooth and nail, Thursday night in the Best First Pet Debate sponsored by the Humane Society of the United States.

"I'll be keeping everyone on a short leash," growled the hard-bitten John McLaughlin, the gruff TV host of his own raucous weekly public affairs show.

He moderated the debate with an urbane wit he no doubt inherited from the late Oliver, his much-loved basset hound, which he praised as a comic genius. McLaughlin vowed to be as doggedly objective as he is in reining in Morton Kondracke or Jack Germond.

"The simple fact is that more people care about pets than presidential politics," he said as he took the podium in the ballroom of Washington's ANA Hotel, a short walk from the White House. "More people care about their pets than any specific issue."

Catty incumbent: *Democrat Bill Clinton's feline, Socks*

Dogged hopeful: *Republican Bob Dole's schnauzer, Leader. Will guard, protect, defend.*

93

THE
FIRST PE

Best First Pet Debate: Cat or Dog, on October 17, 1996, at a big hotel in Washington.

Marine Captain Joseph Trane McCloud from Alexandria, Virginia, escorted me to the event. He and I led a rowdy group of stalwart supporters as we marched down the street to the hotel.

We had to wind our way past spotlights and photographers shouting LEADER! Leader! Look this way!

Captain McCloud

The Washington Post

The Reliable Source
By Ann Gerhart and Annie Groer

Reign of Cats or Dogs?

On Thursday night, one day after President Clinton and Bob Dole have their final face-off, the very loud telepundit John McLaughlin is set to moderate one of the weirder debates of Campaign '96.

"The Best First Pet; Cat or Dog" will be argued by two biped contributing editors at magazines for feline and canine owners, with questions coming from a panel that includes a fifth-grade journalist from My Weekly Reader, the Humane Society of the United States and the publishers of Dog World and Cats Magazine are sponsoring the event at the ANA Hotel on M Street.

Invitations were sent to Socks, the Clinton family kitty, and Leader, the Doles' schnauzer.

No one even inquired if Ross Perot had a pet, let alone requested the company of Honey the golden retriever or any of Perot's cats, goats or horses. "It's just another example of how they are trying to exclude the third party," said a Perot spokeswoman.

© 1996 The Washington Post. Reprinted with permission

GREAT DEBATE

"Cats are great examples of American independence and pride."
Amy Shojai, Contributing Editor, CATS Magazine

Bystanders packed the sidewalk. Some Socks' fans were asking, "Where's Socks?" Do you think I cared?

We all soon learned that the ill-advised Socks was a no show. This oversight on his part was widely booed and not overlooked by the wise judges.

The way I see it, this argument ended before it even started: Whoever heard, *"If you want a friend in Washington get a CAT,"* or *"Man's best friend is a CAT."*

John Cargill
Contributing Editor
DOG WORLD

John McLaughlin, TV Host; Patricia Forkan, Executive Vice President, The Humane Society of the United States; Kendra Fowler, Correspondent, Weekly Reader.

The Humane Society of the United States presents

The GREAT DEBATE
or
The Best FIRST PET

This dramatic poster, created by Washington artist Jim Siemer, is typical of the many contributions made by my friends and supporters during my Internet campaign.

My landslide over Socks was a triumph orchestrated by the powers of the Internet and fueled by the support of friends who never gave up on the potential of a lost little canine.

As you can see, there's more than one way to skin a CAT!

Mr. Keynoter

News of my Paw Poll Victory over Socks spread like wildfire, so no one was surprised when speaking requests came in by mail, phone and fax.

Everyone wanted to hear, step by step, how I had achieved this historic triumph over the incumbent cat.

The traveling, especially the bumper to bumper traffic, was tiring; but *every* speech was standing room only and meeting the crowds gave me a chance to thank all those who voted for me in the Paw Poll.

Watergate Days

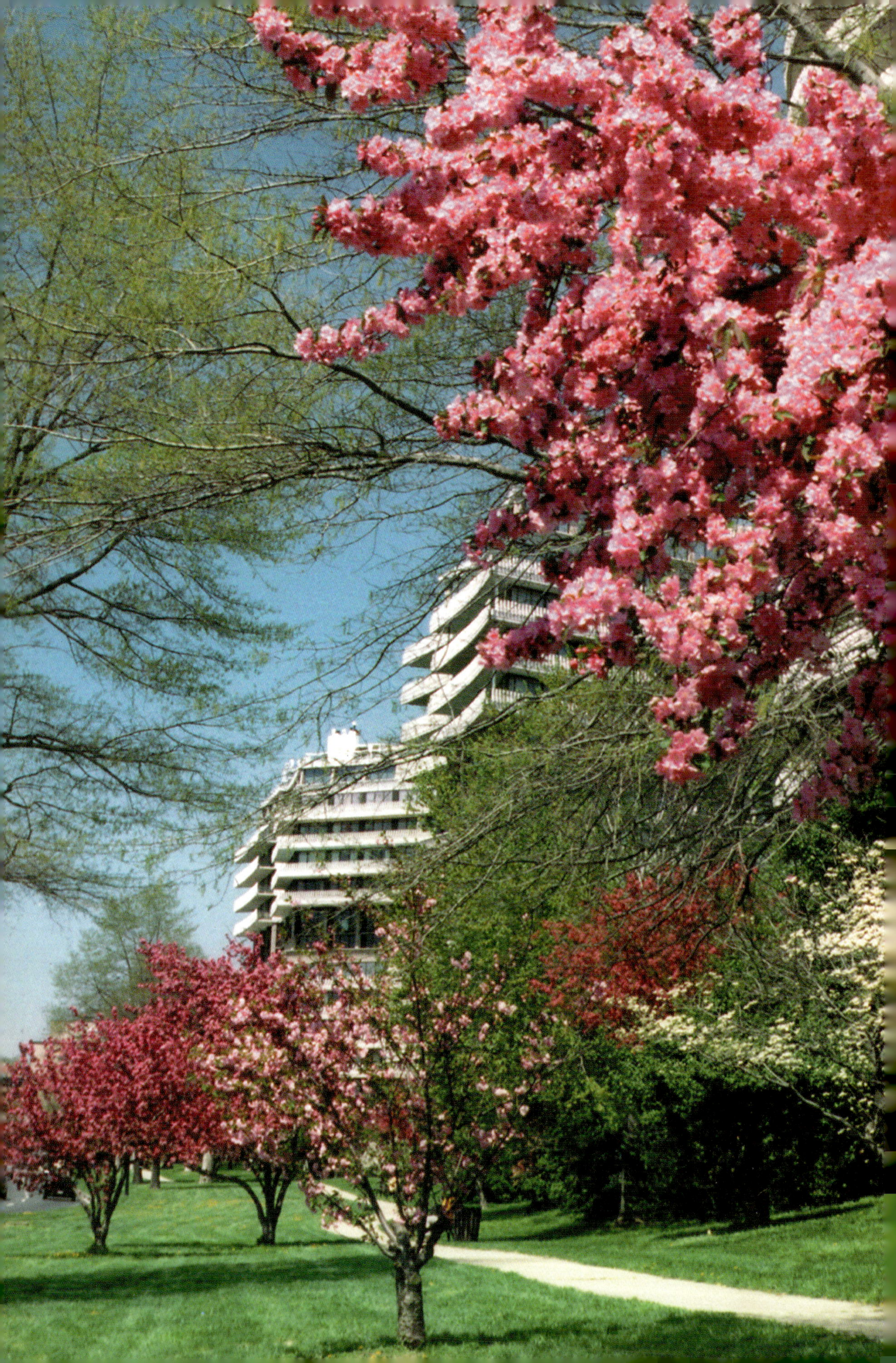

My Backyard

Some observers of the canine condition have suggested that "All dogs are creatures of habit." As for me, I am definitely such a creature. Every day, I wake up at the crack of dawn, take a drink of water and then wait, somewhat impatiently I must admit, in exactly the same place at the patio door. As soon as my human escort arrives, we are on our way. I go from tree to tree, sometimes chasing the errant squirrel or just sniffing along our usual route, which circles Washington's magnificent Watergate complex, right next door to the Kennedy Center. It takes me 30 minutes to cover the four city blocks, or 25 minutes if I take a short-cut through the shopping mall. What I like best about these trips, whether walking down the hall or along the sidewalks outside, is all the cheerful neighbors who wave "Hi" and give me a pat on the back or scratch my ears. I wonder if they know how much their kindness warms my heart.

Our townhouse is in the pet-friendly Watergate South, which is one of the six buildings on the banks of the Potomac River. From a dog's point of view, this is the best of all possible worlds -- 10 acres of green rolling lawns, beautiful flower gardens, intimate rock gardens, and hundreds of flowering trees that bloom each spring. Just imagine – all of this is my backyard!

Through the changing seasons, the Watergate grounds provide a beautiful background for our daily walks.

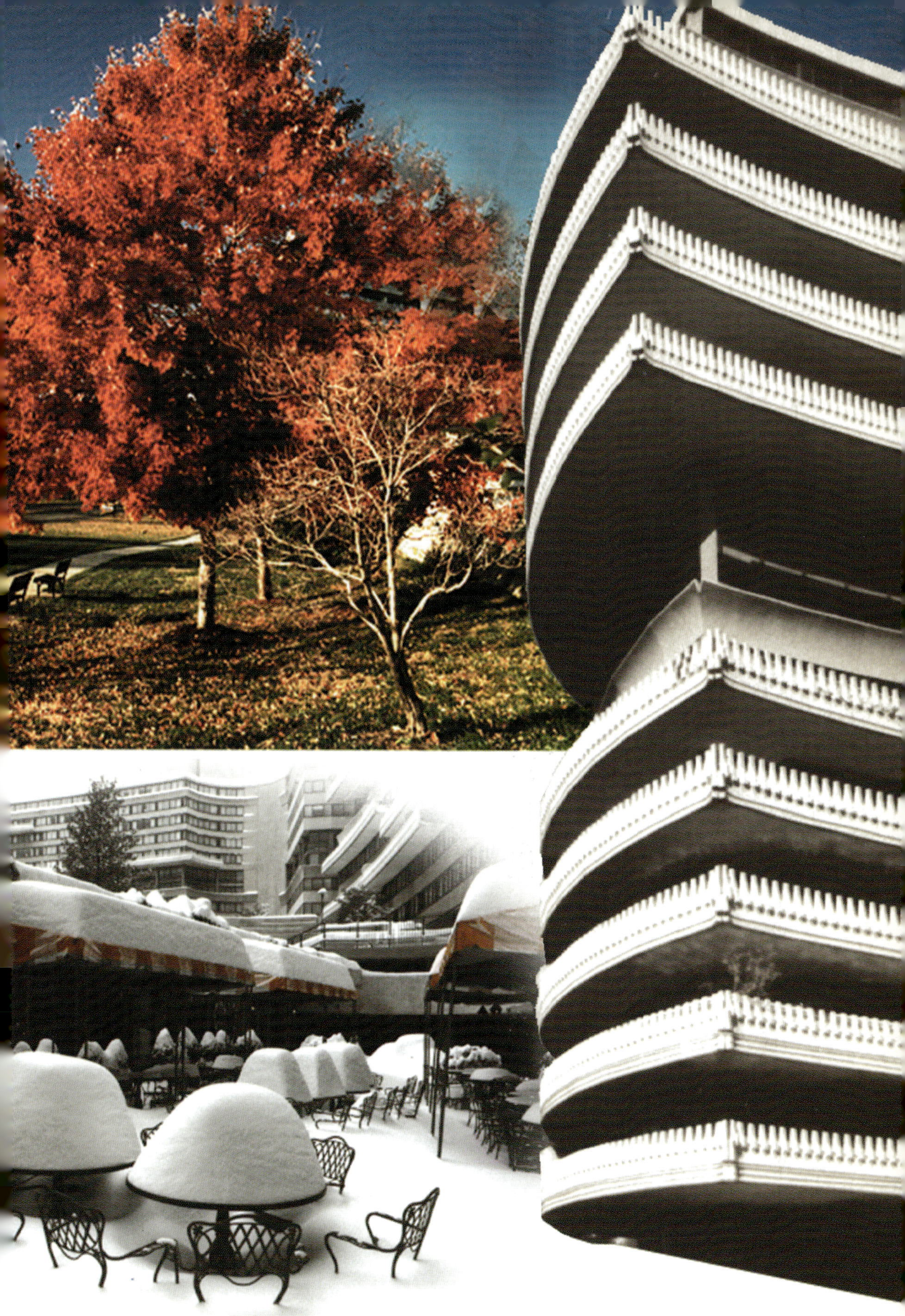

"The Political Animal"

It was no wonder that when USA Network decided to film the story of my life, they started right here at the Watergate. Many movies are made in Washington, but who would have guessed that one would be made about me. The film begins and ends with me sitting beside Bob, my adopted parent, and consists of a series of flashbacks of my adoption, first news conference and the check presentation for the Washington Humane Society. In addition, the producers had to film several more scenes starring me at the Watergate, the White House and the U.S. Senate! Whenever people see my movie, there isn't a dry eye in the place. The show is called *Dog Tales: The Political Animal*, so look out for it when it is shown again on the USA Network.

Our Next-door Neighbor Moves Out

Despite the notoriety of the Watergate address, most of the dogs and humans that live here lead ordinary lives. Some of them, however, attract considerable media attention, and we have become accustomed to seeing reporters and cameras. But nothing prepared us for the events that began on January 21, 1998.

On our 6:30 walk that morning, we noticed several men in trench coats. One identified himself as an ABC news producer and asked if we knew anyone who lived in Apartment 114. Of course we did --- that would be Monica, our next door neighbor!

Thereafter, it wasn't easy to ignore Monica's presence in our building. The entire neighborhood was invaded by satellite trucks, reporters and TV cameramen standing in our driveway or sitting in chairs on the sidewalk or in vans parked nearby. Working in shifts, the media crews made sure that the chairs and vans were always occupied, day and night. All the garage entrances were similarly staked out. This siege lasted until she moved out 9 months later.

As luck would have it, her departure made it possible for us to acquire her unit and double the size of our townhouse. The totally rebuilt apartment gives us a huge kitchen, a fireplace in our living room, a larger dining room, a library-den, and more bedrooms with more closets. But, best of all, more room to exercise, a priority for Elizabeth and Bob, who spend at least 30 minutes daily on the treadmill. Electric machines are off limits to me, so I do my Yoga stretching on the weight lifter.

103

Friends & Family

Buffy & Trixie

JO JO RYAN

Campaigning, 1998. L to R: **Walt Riker** *(now Director, Corporate Communications, McDonalds Restaurants)*; **Elizabeth,** and **Dale Petroskey** *(now President, Baseball Hall of Fame).*

David Sadlier

Harry

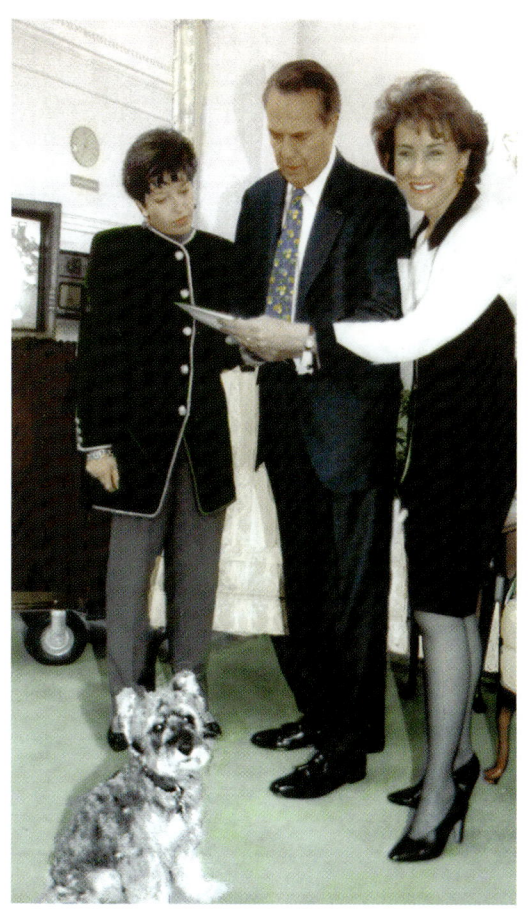

Robin Dole joins her dad and Elizabeth in reviewing the '94 election results.

The venerable **Strom Thurmond** (R-SC). Bob and Senator Thurmond served together in the Senate for nearly thirty years.

The Watergate Bakery does us Proud

Surprise !

    A mystery surrounds the actual date of my birth but I'm told that my teeth indicated that I was two years old when I was rescued—imagine that! Although I have celebrated many birthdays quietly, as number 17 approached, I sensed that something special was in the air. When a beautiful cake arrived from the Watergate Bakery decorated with 17 can-

Party Animal

dles, I didn't need to see the balloons and "Happy Birthday" sign to know that this party was for me.

Chichie, my furdresser, came with her pomeranian, Sable, and arrived early so she could give me a "touch-up." When her paw pals came in (Jelly, the Westie; Nikky, the poodle; and Shadow, the beagle -- all barking and jumping with joy), the party kicked into high gear. We behaved like angels until the food was served, then it was canine chaos. Jelly saved the day when he led a foot race around the patio. Incidentally, the humans had a good time too.

Leader and Jelly

Front row L to R: Jelly Efron, Sable Tescoe, Nikky Ciftci, Shadow Hughes
Back Row L to R: Jean Efron, Mary Vincent, Elizabeth Dole, Chichie Tescoe, Claire Ciftci, Marja Hughes

"He's so dignified"

Heads were about to roll at the WASHINGTON POST when it was scooped by our neighborhood journal, the FOGGY BOTTOM NEWS, with its half-page spread about my birthday party.

Scrambling to recover, the POST immediately contacted my furdresser, for an update on my activities. It was well-known around Washington that no one but Chichie Tescoe had clipped my curly locks for 15 years.

Chichie delivered like a public relations pro. She gave the POST their half-page story, complete with several photos, and anecdotes about yours truly and other well-known Washington pups.

But I'll never forget her remark about me in the last paragraph that almost moved me to tears: "He's so dignified... just like the Senator."

You see—a dog's life isn't so bad, after all.

Two months after completing his memoirs, Leader died on March 1, 1999. He was laid to rest at Noah's Ark Pet Cemetery, Falls Church, Virginia.

Throughout his life he worked to help the Humane Society who rescued him in 1984; so it is to Leader's memory that proceeds from the sale of his book will be donated to the Washington Humane Society.

Additional contributions can be mailed to the Washington Humane Society at 7319 Georgia Avenue, N.W., Washington, DC 20012.

The Washington Post

The Reliable Source

By Ann Gerhart and Annie Groer

Leader: A Life in Politics

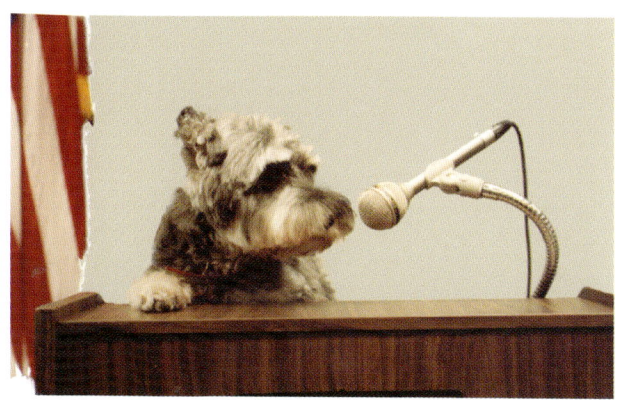

Leader Dole, a low-born friend with lofty goals.

It looks like Leader Dole won't be going on a book tour. His memoirs will be posthumous.

But the schnauzer that Elizabeth Dole rescued from the D.C. Humane Society as a gift for hubby Bob 15 years ago did manage to finish "Follow the Leader: A Dog's Eye View of Washington, D.C." before departing this Earth earlier this month. He was 17; that's 119 in dog years.

In the best tradition of political animals (who among us can forget "Millie's Book" by George and Bar Bush's springer spaniel, or "Dear Socks, Dear Buddy" by Hillary R. Clinton), proceeds from Leader's yet-unpublished book will go to the Washington Humane Society...

© 1999 The Washington Post
Reprinted with permission

Hi...

You don't know me...yet. But I would like to introduce myself --- I'm 9 months old and my name is Leader II.

It was also my good fortune to have been selected to become a member of the Dole family. I will never be able to fill Leader's paw prints but as the years go on I hope to someday go into politics.

Follow me.

*Washington, D. C.
March 2000*

Photo Credits

AP/Wide World Photos, 22

David Adler, 95

Eddie Adams, 31

Harry Benson, 35

P.F. Bentley TIME, 20, 24, 25, 78, 85

Michael J. N Bowles, 34

Cameron Davidson 32

Lynn Bogert Dykstra, Focused Images Photography, Inc., 3, 11, 13, 34-77, 81, 83, 85, 91, 100, 101, 105, 106, 107, 109, 110, 113 Cover

Deborah Feingold / Outline, 33, Back Cover

Judy Foley, 92

John Harrington / Blackstar 40

Ben Man, 97-101

Laura Patterson / ROLLCALL 30

Judd Pilossof, 41

Alan Porter, 19, 84 (Otto)

NBC News Archives, 42

Gay Schackelford, 86, (Spot Bush)

INDEX

Alexander, Claude 40
Ballard, Shirley 15, 27
Batt, Sniffer 81, 82, 89
Bentley, P.F. 25
Bolivar, Simon 67
Boom from Ohio, 81, 88
Buggsy, the Bichon Frise 91
Bungee, 84
Bury, Susan 40
Bush, Spot 81, 86
Bush. Millie 81
Cardinal Hill Imaging 86, 90
Cargill, John 95
Charlie Bear 88
Christensen, Ted 79
Ciftci, Claire 107
  Nikky 107
Cliff, the iguana 81, 84
Clinton, Socks 83, 90, 94, 95, 96
Coats, Sugar 86
Corky 84
Craig, Senator Larry 82
Craig, Pudge 82
David, the cockatiel 90
Davidson, Cameron 32
Douglass, Frederick 47, 48
Dykstra, Lynn Bogert 47
Efron, Jean 107
  Jelly 107
Einstein, Albert 74
Ella from West Virginia 84
Ellis, Charlotte 15, 16
Foley, Schotzie 92
Fordyce, Rainbow 82
Fowler, Kendra 95
Gorton, Brig 82
  Samuel Gorton 82
Gramm, Senator Phil 82
  Gus 82
Healey, Mary 40
Heidi Bear 86
Hughes, Marja 107
Hughes, Shadow 107
Jacco from Australia 91
Jefferson, Thomas 56
Jones, Wilbert 21, 22, 28
Kansas, Charlie 90
Karl, Jonathan 85, 90
King, Larry 36
Khemosabey 81, 84
Leavitt, Mike 86
  Riley 86

Leno, Jay 37
Letterman, David 38
Lieber, 88
Lincoln, Abraham 77
Little Mac, the Sheltie 91
Lucky Boy 84
Lugar, Magnum MG 86
Lugar, Senator and Mrs. 86
McCaffrey, Gen.(Ret.) Barry 44
McCloud, Marine Capt. Joseph Trane 94
McGriff from Canada 90
McLaughlin, John 93, 94, 95
Michelsen, Marianne 91
Miss Taylor 86
Misty, 88
Monica 103
Mr. Tibbs 90
Mulford, Carolyn 33
Nordal, Audun 91
Oftebro, Svein 90
Pataki, Jefferson 86
Patterson, Laura 30
Phoebe, the Dachshund 90
Queenie from Brazil 90
Ridge, Allie & Mollie 82
Ryan, Jo Jo 104
Sadlier, David 105
Samui from Korea 91
Schmidt, Chippy 91
Scott, Willard 42 43
Shayna 86
Shelton, Gen. Hugh 44
Shojai, Amy 95
Siemer, Jim 96
Sorenson, Chad R. 91
Tescoe, Chichie 107, 108
Sable 107
The Humane Society of the U.S 93, 94, 95
Thurmond, Senator Strom 105
USA Network 102
Valentina the Boxer 91
Washington, DC Humane Society 39 40 110 111
Washington, George 58
Weld, Rosie 86
Williams, Mayor Anthony 46
Williamson, Al 91
Ybarra, Shirley 27

News articles reprinted with permission from

Baltimore Sun

Washington Post

People

Time for Kids

US Newswire

Roll Call